1943–44

# COMBAT

# Chindit
## VERSUS
# Japanese Infantryman

Jon Diamond

First published in Great Britain in 2015 by Osprey Publishing,
PO Box 883, Oxford, OX1 9PL, UK
PO Box 3985, New York, NY 10185-3985, USA
E-mail: info@ospreypublishing.com

Osprey Publishing is part of the Osprey Group

A CIP catalogue record for this book is available from the British Library

Print ISBN: 978 1 4728 0651 2
PDF ebook ISBN: 978 1 4728 0652 9
ePub ebook ISBN: 978 1 4728 0653 6

Index by Mark Swift
Typeset in Univers, Sabon and Adobe Garamond Pro
Maps by bounford.com
Originated by PDQ Media, Bungay, UK
Printed in China through Worldprint Ltd

15 16 17 18 19   10 9 8 7 6 5 4 3 2 1

Osprey Publishing is supporting the Woodland Trust, the UK's leading
woodland conservation charity, by funding the dedication of trees.

www.ospreypublishing.com

## Acknowledgements

I am thankful to Neil Grant and the staff and trustees of the Small Arms
School Corps Weapons Collection, as well as the staffs of the United
States Army Military Heritage Institute in Carlisle, Pennsylvania and the
Still Photo Section at the National Archives and Records Administration
in College Park, Maryland. I would also like to thank the editor, Nick
Reynolds, for his marvellous guidance, assistance and meticulous
attention to detail.

## Author's note

In the quoted extracts I have retained the terms 'Jap' and 'Japs', not in any
offensive manner, but only to maintain the authenticity of the extracts. The
use of these terms is in no way intended to convey anything derogatory
about the Japanese soldiers or Japanese people in general. Also, owing to
space limitations, detailed coverage of the Gurkha, West African, Burmese,
American and other Allied combatants involved in the Chindit operations
could not be included in this volume. I would like to acknowledge the vast
and gallant contribution made by these Allied troops in the fight against
the Japanese during the struggle to liberate Burma in World War II.

## Artist's note

Readers may care to note that the original paintings from which the
plates of this book were prepared are available for private sale. All
reproduction copyright whatsoever is retained by the Publishers. All
inquiries should be addressed to:

Peter Dennis, 'Fieldhead', The Park, Mansfield, Nottinghamshire NG18
2AT, UK, or email magie.h@ntlworld.com

The Publishers regret that they can enter into no correspondence upon
this matter.

## Imperial War Museum Collections

Many of the photos in this book come from the Imperial War Museum's
huge collections which cover all aspects of conflict involving Britain and
the Commonwealth since the start of the twentieth century. These rich
resources are available online to search, browse and buy at www.
iwmcollections.org.uk. In addition to Collections Online, you can visit
the Visitor Rooms where you can explore over 8 million photographs,
thousands of hours of moving images, the largest sound archive of its
kind in the world, thousands of diaries and letters written by people in
wartime, and a huge reference library. To make an appointment, call
(020) 7416 5320, or e-mail mail@iwm.org.uk

Imperial War Museum www.iwm.org.uk

| British Army | Indian Army | IJA | US Army |
|---|---|---|---|
| field marshal (FM) | n/a | grand marshal (*Dai-Gensui*) | General of the Army |
| general (Gen) | n/a | marshal general (*Gensui Rikugun Taishō*) | general |
| lieutenant-general (Lt-Gen) | n/a | general (*Rikugun Taishō*) | lieutenant general |
| major-general (Maj-Gen) | n/a | lieutenant-general (*Rikugun Chūjō*) | major general |
| brigadier (Brig) | n/a | major-general (*Rikugun Shōshō*) | brigadier general |
| colonel (Col) | n/a | colonel (*Rikugun Taisa*) | colonel |
| lieutenant-colonel (Lt-Col) | n/a | lieutenant-colonel (*Rikugun Chūsa*) | lieutenant colonel |
| major (Maj) | n/a | major (*Rikugun Shōsa*) | major |
| captain (Capt) | subedar major | captain (*Rikugun Taii*) | captain |
| lieutenant (Lt) | subedar | 1st lieutenant (*Rikugun Chūi*) | 1st lieutenant |
| 2nd lieutenant (2/Lt) | jemadar | 2nd lieutenant (*Rikugun Shōi*) | 2nd lieutenant |
| regimental sergeant major (RSM) | regimental havildar major | warrant officer (*Rikugun Jun-i*) | n/a |
| company sergeant major (CSM) | company havildar major | n/a | n/a |
| n/a | n/a | n/a | master sergeant |
| n/a | n/a | n/a | first sergeant |
| n/a | n/a | n/a | technical sergeant |
| staff sergeant (S/Sgt) | n/a | sergeant Major (*Sōchō*) | staff sergeant |
| sergeant (Sgt) | havildar | sergeant (*Gunsō*) | sergeant |
| corporal (Cpl) | naik | corporal (*Gochō*) | corporal |
| n/a | n/a | junior corporal (*Gochō Kimmu jōtōhei*) | n/a |
| lance corporal (L/Cpl) | lance naik | lance corporal (*Heichō*) | n/a |
| n/a | n/a | senior private (*Jōtōhei*) | n/a |
| n/a | n/a | acting senior private (*Jōtōhei Kimmusha*) | n/a |
| n/a | n/a | private first class (*Ittōhei*) | private first class |
| n/a | n/a | private second class (*Nitōhei*) | n/a |
| private/fusilier/rifleman | rifleman | recruit | private |

# CONTENTS

# Introduction

On the evening of 2 March 1943, only days after the first Chindit operation in Japanese-occupied Burma had commenced, Maj Arthur Emmett's No. 2 Column was bivouacking a couple of miles west of the railway station at Kyaikthin in anticipation of the next day's attack to blow it up. Emmett's scouts observed that two trains had arrived at the Kyaikthin railway station during that afternoon, but the Chindits were completely unaware that these trains contained roughly 800 Japanese soldiers of the 215th Infantry Regiment (33rd Division). At 2200hrs, Lt Ian MacHorton was near the rear of a column of 250 men and 20 mules as it trekked down the railway-line embankment. The Japanese, hidden in the jungle some 20yd beyond the embankment, were making their final ambush preparations. As MacHorton recounted after the war:

There came the sound of just one bang up at the front somewhere beyond my vision. But only for a split second, then an inferno of noise engulfed the world around me! Then came the high-pitched staccato scream of a machine-gun … Then overwhelmingly many more machine-guns joined in an ear-splitting chorus. The crash–ping of rifles and banging grenades, joined in to swell the noise of sudden battle to a fearful crescendo. Somewhere ahead there was an uncertain scuffling. A hoarse voice cried: 'Take cover!' and another screamed 'Christ Almighty!' and was silenced. (Quoted in Chinnery 2010: 62)

The brutal, sustained combat that characterized the Chindits' operations in Burma in 1943 and 1944 had its roots in the lightning Japanese conquest of Burma in 1942. For the Western Allies, the reconquest of northern Burma – along with the capture of the vital communications hub at Myitkyina on the Irrawaddy River – was of paramount importance. This was in order to re-open the old Burma Road to the south-western provinces of China, thereby keeping Chiang Kai-shek's forces in the war fighting against the Imperial Japanese Army (IJA). The British High Command, however, did not want to resume the offensive in the harsh terrain of northern Burma. The British approach was made clear by the comments of Lt-Gen Noel Irwin, GOC-in-C Eastern Army, who stated while answering reporters' questions that 'in Japan the infantryman is the *corps d'élite*, while the British put our worst men into the infantry' (quoted in Hastings 2011: 420).

At first, the Japanese also believed that northern Burma was unsuitable as a base for conducting offensive operations. In September 1942 Lieutenant-General Mutaguchi Renya, commander of 18th Division, told Lieutenant-General Iida Shōjirō, the commander of 15th Army, that the terrain in northern Burma, with its endless jungles and mountains, was so formidable that his division would be unable to cross the mountains into Assam or be supported there. This stymied a 15th Army preliminary plan to advance through the Hukawng Valley and on to Assam's air depots in a bid to sever Chiang Kai-shek's air supply route, called the 'Hump'. By early 1943 the Japanese forces in Burma comprised 15th Army, headquartered in Rangoon; it was composed of four IJA divisions, among them 18th and 33rd divisions (Lieutenant-General Sakurai Shōzō, later Lieutenant-General Yanangida Motoso), which were deployed facing to the north and west in order to hold northern Burma and the Chindwin River with a skeleton force of only one or two battalions, while the other battalions re-fitted and recuperated after their conquest of Burma.

In 1943–44, Brig, later Maj Gen, Orde Wingate – a military maverick and proponent of guerrilla warfare – would teach Mutaguchi that a large force could successfully cross the hills and Chindwin River separating India and Burma. Wingate was summoned by his mentor, FM Sir Archibald P. Wavell – C-in-C India – to utilize Wingate's newly evolving tactic of Long Range

Japanese infantryman and his bicycle with full kit on the back fender and handlebars during the Burmese invasion in the spring of 1942. The Burmese offensive ended with the defeat of the bulk of British and Indian forces in Burma at Kalewa, on the Chindwin River, near the Indian border, with nearly the entire country having been captured by the IJA by May 1942 at the cost of 2,000 fatalities. The Japanese advanced across Burma for more than 100 days and trekked across 1,500 miles, advancing on average 30 miles a day. According to Tsuji, 'During the latter half of 1941 the armies which were to become engaged in southern areas abandoned their horses and were reorganized into mixed formations using bicycles' (Tsuji 1997: 10). The load that could be carried strapped to the handlebars and rear fender of a bicycle was much less than that carried by a pack animal, so throughout the Malayan campaign, the Burmese conquest and even 1944's Operation *U-Go*, the Japanese infantry would be directed to utilize captured enemy supplies and ammunition. (USAMHI)

**MAP KEY**

**1  8 February 1943:** At the start of *Operation Longcloth*, Wingate's 3,000-strong 77th Indian Infantry Brigade embarks before crossing the Chindwin River undetected and advancing along the operational boundary between the Japanese 18th and 33rd divisions. On 6 March, Maj J.M. 'Mike' Calvert's No. 3 Column will ambush and defeat a Japanese force comprised of elements of I Battalion, 55th Infantry Regiment (I/55th Infantry) at Nankan Station.

**2  4 March 1943:** Having completed their demolition tasks and crossed the Irrawaddy River, the men of 77th Indian Infantry Brigade's Northern Group begins dispersing for India. Numbering 2,200 men – comprised of Brigade HQ, the Burma Rifles HQ and HQ 2 Group, as well as Nos 3, 4, 5, 7 and 8 columns – Northern Group has trekked between Pinbon and Pinlebu towards their primary target, the railway running north–south between Wuntho and Indaw.

**3  24 March 1943:** Having also crossed the Irrawaddy, 77th Indian Infantry Brigade's Southern Group is ordered to head to the Kachin Hills. Composed of HQ 1 Group along with Nos 1 and 2 columns, Southern Group has acted as a diversionary body, with its target destination being the railway near Kyaikthin. By the first week of June 1943, 2,180 Chindits will have returned to India, often in small groups, of the just over 3,000 Chindits that entered Burma. The remaining Chindits either died or became prisoners of war.

**4  5/6 March 1944:** During the night, Operation *Thursday*, with its extensive 1st Air Commando Group component, begins, with 77th Indian Infantry Brigade being airlifted by glider from airfields at Lalaghat and Hailekandi to the 'Broadway' landing field.

**5  6–7 March 1944:** A second glider-borne operation begins: to fly – by glider – the advance guard of 111th Indian Infantry Brigade into 'Chowringhee', a landing zone some 50 miles to the south-west of Broadway, between the Shweli and Irrawaddy rivers. Large elements of this brigade will march north-west across the Irrawaddy to the vicinity of Baumauk to provide assistance for 16th British Infantry Brigade, which arrives in the Indaw area on 20 March having set out on its foot-march from Ledo on 5 February.

**6  8 March–2 July 1944:** After invading India's Assam province by crossing the Chindwin River, 15th Army (Lieutenant-General Mutaguchi Renya), comprised of 15th, 31st and 33rd divisions, is embroiled in a life-and-death struggle against Lt-Gen William Slim's British and Indian forces. The Japanese are defeated at Imphal (8 March–3 July) and Kohima (4 April–22 June).

**7  9 March 1944:** Brig Calvert takes five columns of 77th Indian Infantry Brigade from Broadway to set up a railway and motor-road block at Henu, and clashes with IJA forces there at the battle of Pagoda Hill on 17–18 March 1944. This 'stronghold'/block will be called 'White City'. After Wingate's death on 24 March, Brig W.D.A. 'Joe' Lentaigne is promoted to acting major-general and assumes command of all Chindit brigades, although they are under the overall direction of Lt Gen Joseph W. Stilwell.

**8  2–12 June 1944:** With the advent of the spring monsoon season and the non-sustainability of Chindit airfields at their 'strongholds', Calvert takes his 77th Indian Infantry Brigade to capture Mogaung; 3rd West African, 14th British and 111th Indian Infantry brigades also move northwards to assist Stilwell's Sino-American advance into the Mogaung Valley and Myitkyina. Calvert's capture of Mogaung, the last major Chindit operation, is successfully completed on 27 June, although it decimates his brigade as a fighting unit. In August 1944 the exhausted survivors of 3rd West African, 14th British, 77th Indian and 111th Indian Infantry brigades finally return to India after five gruelling months of campaigning.

Penetration (LRP) to disrupt the enemy's lines of communication (LOC) in Burma. Wavell had noted in his diary that 'I have twice used Wingate … for unorthodox campaigns [Palestine and Ethiopia]' (quoted in Diamond 2012a: 62). Both Wavell and Wingate knew that a different type of British infantryman was required for this role; one indoctrinated with special training and physical conditioning, to re-enter the jungles and mountains of northern Burma. Along with a new martial spirit, newly promoted Brig Wingate's 'Chindit' (a mispronunciation of the Burmese word for the jungle's fiercest animal, the lion, *Chinthe*), would also possess radio communications to summon Royal Air Force (RAF) resupply by air, allowing his force to penetrate deeply within the enemy's interior. Burma's jungle canopy and mountains would obscure his force's movements and, thus, would provide a perfect theatre to test LRP methods to disrupt Japanese LOC.

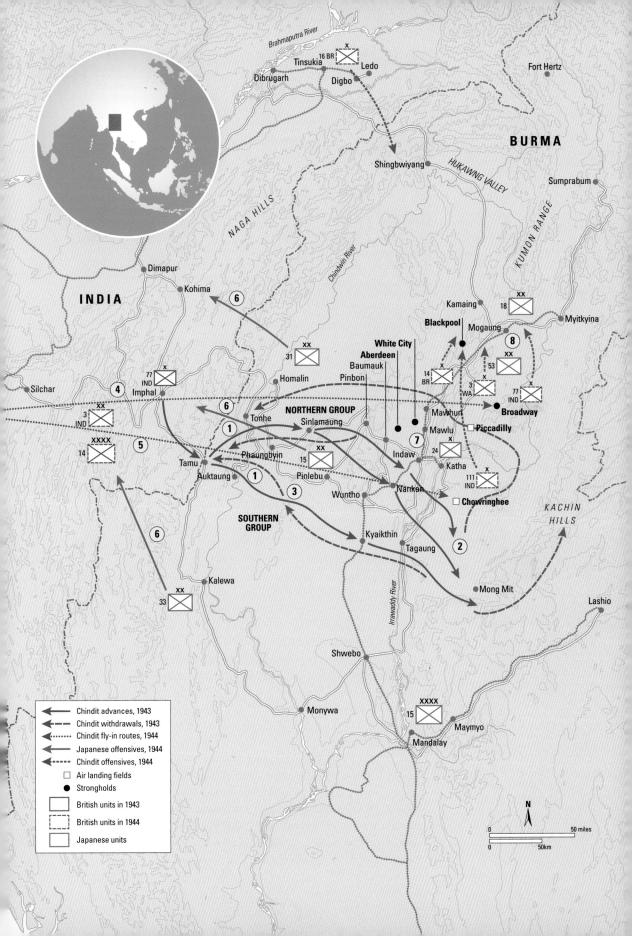

Brahmaputra River

Tinsukia
Dibrugarh
Digbo
16 BR x
Ledo
Fort Hertz

**BURMA**

Shingbwiyang
HUKAWNG VALLEY
Sumprabum

NAGA HILLS

Chindwin River

KUMON RANGE

Dimapur
Kohima ⑥

INDIA

Kamaing
Mogaung 18 xx
Myitkyina
**Blackpool** ⑧
53 xx

Silchar
77 IND x
Imphal ④
31 xx
Homalin
⑥
Tonhe ⑥
① Sinlamaung
**NORTHERN GROUP**
Baumauk
Pinbon
**White City**
**Aberdeen**
Mawhun
14 BR x
3 WA x
77 IND x
**Broadway**

3 IND xx
14 xxxx ⑤
Tamu
Phaungbyin
① Pinlebu
Auktaung ①
15 xx
③
Indaw ⑦
Mawlu x
24
Katha
□ **Piccadilly**
**KACHIN HILLS**
Wuntho
Nankan
111 IND x
□ **Chowringhee**

**SOUTHERN GROUP**
Kyaikthin
Tagaung
②
Mong Mit
Lashio

⑥
Kalewa
33 xx

Irrawaddy River

Shwebo
Monywa
15 xxxx
Maymyo
Mandalay

N

0        50 miles
0    50km

Brig Wingate is pictured during Operation *Longcloth* instructing his Chindit officers in the field. These informal sessions enabled Wingate to espouse his tactics for jungle victory over the IJA, which was up until then near-unthinkable for British troops. Wingate's LRP experiment was to be tested by the Chindits during *Longcloth* to overcome the Allied perception of the IJA infantryman's jungle invincibility after defeats in Burma and Malaya. Hit-and-run methods disrupting Japanese LOC; use of the jungle for cover and evasion; and a column-sized combat infantry unit for mobility, were Wingate's tenets. At the far left is Signaller Eric Hutchins, who operated a vital air–ground wireless set. Wingate preached that his troops would not have to depend on a land LOC as long as efficient wireless units were employed to signal supply-dropping points accurately to transport aircraft. Wingate envisaged his force penetrating deeply into Japanese-held territory to disrupt their LOC out of proportion to the size of his Chindit columns. (USAMHI)

Operation *Longcloth* commenced in February 1943 and was intended to disrupt Japanese LOC, principally by destroying large portions of the railway to the west of the Irrawaddy River. After that, Wingate intended to move 77th Indian Infantry Brigade across the Irrawaddy to further disrupt Japanese LOC on the Salween River front, in conjunction with Chinese forces that were to advance east from Yunnan Province. Operation *Longcloth* was to test whether Wingate's newly trained infantryman could challenge and overcome the known prowess of the IJA foot-soldier, who up until this point 'owned' the Burmese jungles and mountains. The Chindit LRP mission in 1943 was also intended to reduce the pressure of a Japanese offensive against Sumprabum, from where Kachin tribesmen led by a handful of British officers were waging a guerrilla conflict against the IJA. Since other planned Allied offensives in the region that would have coincided with Operation *Longcloth* were cancelled, Wingate had to plead his case to Wavell to allow the mission to continue as planned. According to Wavell,

> I had to balance the inevitable losses – the larger since there would be no other operations to divide the enemy's forces – to be sustained without strategical profit, against the experience to be gained of Wingate's new method and organization. I had little doubt in my own mind of the proper course, but I had to satisfy myself also that Wingate had no doubts and that the enterprise had a good chance of success and would not be a senseless sacrifice. (Quoted in Diamond 2012b: 32)

# The Opposing Sides

## ORIGINS, RECRUITMENT AND TRAINING

The origins of Wingate's Chindits and the Japanese infantrymen of 18th Division were very different. Wingate's initial command was formed as an *ad hoc* brigade from a wide cross-section of British, Empire and Dominion personnel, including many older conscripted Britons, young, inexperienced Gurkha volunteers and indigenous Chin, Karen and Kachin tribesmen, led by British and Indian Army officers with varying levels of experience and expertise. Recruited from certain districts of Kyushu, 18th Division was a much more homogenous formation; this immediately contributed to a strong bond among the conscripts (average age 19), who shared a sense of commitment to honouring their families.

For transport, Wingate would revert to pack animals such as elephants, bullocks and – most importantly – mules. Here, a mule stands ready to be loaded with an RAF radio or disassembled 3in mortar. Mules from Argentina and the United States were preferred to the smaller Indian ones. (USAMHI)

Both sides strove to prepare their soldiers for the rigours of the fighting in Burma, but the approach they took to this in the face of shared threats posed by the terrain and the climate often differed substantially. Doctrinally, a sharp contrast existed between the British Chindit and his Japanese opponent with respect to the amount of initiative required of the ordinary soldier. Strict obedience to superiors and very limited individual initiative were demanded of the Japanese infantryman; in contrast, in order for Wingate's dispersal and rendezvous tactics to be successful every individual Chindit infantryman had to display initiative and learn how to survive alone or in a small group, especially if his officer or NCO (non-commissioned officer) were killed or wounded.

Chindits practise using canoes in India during the autumn of 1943. Since Burmese rivers would need to be crossed during Operation *Longcloth* and at times the Chindits' performance during *Longcloth* was patchy – with much loss of men, mules and supplies – Wingate decided to augment Chindit training in small craft skills for 1944's Operation *Thursday*. Training was conducted with a variety of watercraft including RAF dinghies, canoes and improvised tug ferries. In late 1942, Wingate's 77th Indian Infantry Brigade had been quartered at Saugor, near Jhansi, in the Central Provinces of India, many miles from the nearest road and – as he intended – located squarely in the jungle just as the monsoons erupted. He intended to train his men in jungle warfare amid conditions as gruelling as anything they might encounter in the forthcoming campaign, until every Chindit became a self-reliant, toughened and cunning jungle fighter conversant with fieldcraft for survival in order to defeat the Japanese. Intensive training was essential, to make men respond instinctively to emergencies. Wingate placed these combat virtues at the heart of his Chindit doctrine and training. (USAMHI)

# British

Wingate formed his original Chindits as 77th Indian Infantry Brigade in July 1942. The Chindits never enjoyed a designated recruitment process; Wingate was given 13th Battalion, The King's (Liverpool Regiment) as a nucleus for his brigade. These troops were allotted to Wingate because they were the only ones available at the time. Most had lived in large urban centres such as Manchester and Liverpool, and the average age was over 30. Ultimately, approximately 40 per cent of 13th King's would be transferred away from Wingate's command, but the majority remained to become Chindits. Prior to Operation *Longcloth*, Wingate wrote: 'If ordinary family men from Liverpool and Manchester can be trained for this specialized jungle war behind the enemy's lines, then any fit man in the British Army can be trained to do the same, and we show ourselves to the world as fighting men second to none, which I believe we are' (quoted in Burchett 1944: 179).

Some elements of the force, however, were far more suited to the rigours of the campaigns ahead, such as Maj Michael Calvert's 142 Commando Company, which had served during the British retreat from Burma and had received demolition training at Maymyo's Bush Warfare School. In addition to training the infantrymen, Wingate and his officers had to ensure the accompanying RAF volunteers understood the intricacies of air supply and radio communications since this was a cornerstone tenet of Wingate's LRP strategy. Unlike his Japanese counterparts, Wingate was able to get reinforcements (new officers, NCOs and volunteers) for his existing units after the significant culling of the unfit within his ranks. The Chindit NCOs initially came from the existing units assigned to Wingate, but the influx of volunteers once the formation was established strengthened the numbers of these vital junior leaders.

In February 1943, Wingate asserted that there were three elements that made up a good soldier: physical toughness; training, in which were included intelligence and education, which alone ensured adaptability and grasp; and courage. This last element, the most important, he defined as the power to endure present evil for the sake of ultimate good. Wingate believed that a hardened, well-trained soldier needed far less courage than a soft and ignorant one. When not on forced marches, a training day began at 0800hrs with 30 minutes of bayonet drill and unarmed combat. Junglecraft lectures were delivered after the morning meal, along with training in the use of the compass, and map-reading skills. Due to the extreme heat, much of the afternoon was spent resting before doing late-afternoon work assignments such as clearing jungle for mule lines. Calvert justified the intensity of the training programme: 'Most soldiers never realized that they could do the things they did, and hardly believe it now. One advantage of exceptionally hard training is that it proves to a man what he can do and suffer' (Calvert 1996: 10). The men were often thirsty,

bitten by insects and leeches and pushed to exhaustion during this process, but the rigours of training in the jungles of the Central Provinces proved effective in preparing the Chindits for the hardships ahead of them. One Chindit, Philip Stibbe, commented, 'we all knew how to live and move in the jungle; we all had a pretty good idea of the special tactics we were going to employ and every man in the column had some idea about how to use a map and compass, a skill which was later to save many lives' (Stibbe 1997: 25).

## Japanese

The Imperial Japanese Army's 18th Division garrisoned the area through which Wingate's Chindit columns would operate during 1943 and 1944. According to one of those who served with it, Private Fujino Hideo, 'The *Kiku* [18th Division] was outstanding as the pick of the IJA' (Fujino 1964: i). Having seen heavy fighting in China, 18th Division had accumulated as much operational experience by the end of 1941 as most Anglo-American divisions would acquire in the entire 1939–45 war. Although 18th Division was logistically 'fatigued' by mid-February 1942, having done the bulk of forced marching through the Malayan jungle along the eastern coast of the Malay Peninsula, the expansiveness of the Burmese geography demanded hard-driving troops capable of near-ceaseless marching for patrolling and garrisoning forward outposts. Once established in Burma, however, the division would suffer from attrition, with few replacements for battlefield casualties being made available.

In theory, his training prepared the Japanese infantryman well for war in tropical environments. During the 1930s, the IJA maintained a large garrison on the island of Formosa and founded a jungle-warfare school there at which techniques for jungle combat were perfected, including minor nuances such as issuing headbands to soldiers to keep the sweat from pouring into their eyes while aiming their rifles, as well as major improvements such as utilizing lighter weapons and loads for the hot, steamy climate. Proper approaches to matters as diverse as combatting diseases such as malaria, and weapons maintenance in

A typical pre-war Japanese conscription class group photograph. The Japanese infantryman entered the military conscription system at the age of 19 and was assigned to a specific class dependent on his capabilities. Japan had the most draconian conscription and reserve system of all the major powers during World War II. On 7 December 1941, the IJA extended regular enlistments to three years, and only granted exemptions to skilled technicians in critical wartime occupations, such as the aviation industry, arsenals and munitions factories. Failure to make the highest grade as a recruit would bring dishonour on the conscript and his family. Conversely, being appointed to the first grade in the troop class gave one's family much to celebrate, while – initially – not being consigned to the first classes often resulted in a social stigma; however, this waned as manpower needs became ever more onerous after the major territorial gains following the lightning victories over the Western Allies in the Pacific and South Asia. The men of 18th Division were conscripted peasants from the Nagasaki and Fukuoka areas of Kyushu, one of the home Japanese islands, which was noted for producing a robust and bellicose warrior. These soldiers fulfilled the dictum that peasants often make the most stoical riflemen. Unlike his Western counterpart, by the time a Japanese conscript arrived at his regiment to begin his term of service, he had already received a significant amount of military training, and was very well prepared for the rigours of military life. (USAMHI)

IJA units strove to instil fighting élan in their newly arrived conscripts through close-combat training, with significant time being spent on bayonet fighting and hand-to-hand combat. The bayonet or *juken* was as important to the aspiring IJA infantryman as the sword was to the samurai warrior. Not only was the bayonet's use a major part of IJA combat tactics, but it was also an integral element of the infantryman's warrior code. Consistent with that tenet, the Japanese bayonet was never shortened during the war, as they were frequently among other warring armies, and were maintained at 20in until the conflict's end. Here, Japanese infantry undertake bayonet practice, which also often occurred during off-duty hours. Unfortunately, in China and in other conquered locales, bayonet practice was not always done using sacks filled with straw. (USAMHI)

humid conditions were also explored. At the start of 1941, Lieutenant-Colonel Tsuji Masanobu, a highly regarded staff officer at 25th Army headquarters, joined the research unit in Formosa as its commander. His researchers prepared a pamphlet, *Read This Alone and the War Can Be Won*, which summarized their findings and was approved by Japanese Imperial General Headquarters (Warren 2007: 51). Suggestions such as 'wearing clothing as loose as possible to allow the air to circulate and it is a good idea to carry a fan' were typically practical hints in the soldiers' guidebook (quoted in Smith 2006: 68).

A spartan training regime was devised to demonstrate that the Japanese infantryman could overcome many, if not all, of nature's obstacles. To prove that the infantryman's spirit glowed hotter than Japan's summer heat, soldiers practised bayonet drilling in the mid-afternoon heat. To show an indifference to the cold, units during training would march through freezing streams in winter. Since this was to be a foot-mobile army, the IJA soldiers marched for tens of miles in conditioning marches. To demonstrate that the infantryman disregarded fatigue, conscripts would complete their long conditioning marches with double laps and if a soldier fell out, he was beaten severely. IJA conscripts suffered the harsh reality of basic training with frequent beatings by veterans and marches that would push one's level of endurance. Deep down, the conscript knew that this physical intimidation, bordering on dehumanization, might ultimately save his life, by keeping him on his feet during a gruelling march rather than falling behind. After mastering the skills instilled during training, the recruit (a private second class) would be promoted to private first class after six months with the regiment.

In May, June and July each year, infantry units trained at squad, platoon and company level. Endurance was the key to these exercises, since the IJA believed that offensive action, rapid marching over long distances, and surprise gained by night attacks were the essential elements of tactical success. The infantrymen practised moving in concentrated formations to optimize both control and morale. Night attacks provided IJA units some safety in avoiding strong enemy defensive fire, as it was more difficult to use supporting arms effectively in the dark. Night training concentrated on individual skills such as noise prevention, navigation and trail marking. Training would culminate with the autumn grand manoeuvres, attended by the Emperor.

## COMBAT DOCTRINE AND ORGANIZATION

British and Japanese approaches to doctrine and its implementation also differed sharply. For the former, the Burmese jungle terrain was to be used as protective cover for marching and manoeuvring. Wingate was convinced that the jungle canopy would be his ally, enabling him to hide the trek of his columns and also provide an ideal setting for dispersal to evade the enemy further if unwanted contact was made with a larger enemy patrol.

# British

In Operation *Longcloth*, Wingate intended to use his Chindits to conduct ambushes behind Japanese lines, exploiting the Chindits' mobility and ability to disperse into the vastness of the Burmese jungle to evade the Japanese. This was very different from the methods used by conventional British Army and Indian Army units in the Far East. To achieve this, Wingate's operational element for both of his Burmese invasions was the 'column'. Each column, numbering about 400 men, consisted of: a headquarters; a Burma Rifles reconnaissance platoon; a demolition or commando squad; an infantry company of four platoons; a support platoon equipped with two 3in mortars and two Vickers machine guns; a mule transport platoon; an air liaison detachment composed of an RAF officer and radio operators; a doctor and two orderlies; and a radio detachment for communication between and within columns. There was no heavy transport, and mules carried the heavier equipment. Since aerial supply was of paramount importance, an RAF signal section was attached to each column to direct Allied aircraft to suitable parachute dropping zones, which were always under the threat of IJA fighters based at Myitkyina and other Burmese airfields.

For Operation *Thursday*, Wingate's core element of 3rd Indian Infantry Division, or Special Force, was formed at Jhansi on 18 September 1943. For this second LRP operation, Wingate was to get six brigades, including three from the British 70th Infantry Division and one from 81st (West Africa) Division. Brig Calvert commanded 77th Indian Infantry Brigade, composed of 1st Battalion, The King's (Liverpool Regiment), 1st Battalion, The Lancashire Fusiliers, 1st Battalion, The South Staffordshire Regiment, 3rd Battalion, 6th Gurkha Rifles and 3rd Battalion, 9th Gurkha Rifles. Brig Lentaigne led 111th Indian Infantry Brigade with 2nd Battalion, The King's Own Royal Regiment and 1st Battalion, The Cameronians as its core. Brig Bernard Fergusson commanded 16th British Infantry Brigade, which was composed of 2nd Battalion, The Queen's Royal Regiment (West Surrey), 2nd Battalion, The Leicestershire Regiment, and elements of the Royal Artillery and the Royal Armoured Corps. The 14th British and 23rd Indian Infantry brigades were made up of men from the former British 70th Division, a veteran, battle-hardened formation with long Middle East experience; Wingate obtained these troops despite the protestations of General Headquarters at New Delhi, which wanted to keep this infantry division intact. The sixth and final brigade was Brig A.H.G. Ricketts's 3rd West African Infantry Brigade, which had arrived in India in November 1943. All told, Special Force numbered about 23,000 men by mid-March 1944.

The novel aspect of Wingate's LRP doctrine for Operation *Thursday* was to establish defended areas ('strongholds') wherever his brigades were operating. The British entry into Burma would now be made by C-47 Dakota aircraft and Waco gliders. An initial group of roughly two glider-

Members of a Chindit column march in single file through tall grass. Although offering concealment, this terrain was difficult to trek through, especially for the pack animals transporting the heavier equipment such as the radios. For Operation *Longcloth*, the Chindits' trek through the dense, hot, humid jungle was accompanied by torrential rain, deep mud, dense bamboo thickets, leeches, ants, spiders and other predatory animals. A typical day's march would start just before dawn and was divided into one-hour stages. During a march, each column was divided into four platoons, and the Chindits bivouacked as separate platoons providing their own defence perimeter. Officers and men ate and slept together. Wingate preached that a column's security was its mobility and ability to disperse and regroup if confronted by larger enemy forces. However, once the fog of war descended during combat, dispersal frequently resulted in chaos, when it proved impossible to brief everyone on the rendezvous to which every man should head. (USAMHI)

This plate shows a British corporal in his mid-to late 20s as he readies his Bren light machine gun to fire at attacking Japanese infantry from a prepared ambush site just north of the Nankan railway station in northern Burma during Operation *Longcloth*. A Liverpudlian, he is 5ft 6in tall and weighs only 130lb having marched into Burma in early February 1943, explaining his bearded and unkempt appearance.

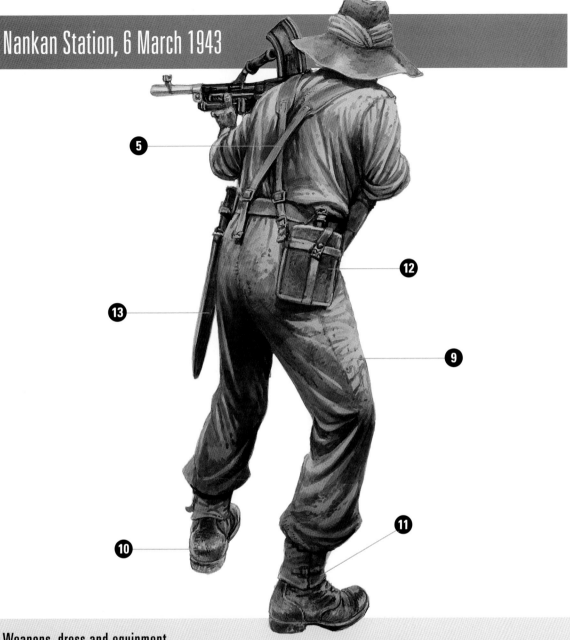

## Weapons, dress and equipment

This Chindit is armed with the Bren Mk II light machine gun (**1**) with its bipod (**2**) folded back. This gun, based on a proven Czechoslovakian design, the ZB vz.26, provided accurate automatic firepower at 500 rounds per minute. It proved to be quite durable and relatively light at 22.5lb, enabling it to be fired from the hip, with a relatively short overall length of 45.25in and an effective range of over 1,000yd. The Bren's box magazine (**3**) usually contained 30 rounds of .303in ammunition. Additional magazines were carried in canvas ammunition pouches on his waist (**4**), which were secured to his standard 1937-pattern webbing equipment; dyed green for jungle camouflage, it fitted over both shoulders and crossed the back (**5**).

This soldier wears the bush or slouch hat (**6**), which was officially introduced in 1942 to replace the Wolseley helmet and pith hat; it was cool and provided shaded vision. A cloth *puggaree* (**7**) encircles the brim of the hat. He wears an Indian-made four-pocket bush shirt (**8**) worn

here tucked inside his British-made 'Khaki Drill Long' trousers (**9**) that have been dyed jungle green. Above the Indian-made 'ammunition' boots (**10**), he wears the Indian-made web anklets (**11**), which have shorter web fastening straps than their British-made counterparts.

Since this Chindit is at a pre-arranged ambush, he has shed much of his gear and packs. When on the march, a small haversack and a steel-framed Everest backpack would be carried to stow his heavy load (up to 60lb) of rations, mess equipment, spare clothing and boots, grenades, mosquito netting, groundsheet and cape, and personal items. An Indian-made water bottle within a canvas carrier (**12**) is suspended from his webbing and worn over the right hip. Vital to hack through some of northern Burma's dense vegetation, a machete (**13**) carried in a standard leather scabbard is worn over the left hip. All in all, this combat load weighs roughly 35lb.

During training, Chindits had undergone lengthy marches through Indian terrain that was representative of Burma's jungles and waterways. Chindit forced marches were often greater than 50 miles in distance, starting before dawn and trekking in single file, a mile and a quarter long, for six hours with only two short breaks. At 1100hrs, the march was halted for food and more rest. The march continued at 1600hrs, when the temperatures were beginning to decline, until 1800hrs for another brief break. The forced march resumed until the next day's dawn with a ten-minute break every two hours. Wingate marched on foot along with his troops, even though horses were available and the brigadier was an excellent horseman. (USAMHI)

borne columns (approximately 800 men in total) would occupy a field that would be converted into a landing strip for the larger transport aircraft to air-ferry in the remaining columns of the brigades. Wingate envisaged that these defended areas or 'strongholds' would be ready to disrupt Japanese installations and LOC. The 'stronghold' would enable columns to set out on raids from its perimeter and to retire into it for safety. With supply and relief, these 'strongholds' could tie down as many Japanese personnel as a conventional Allied offensive.

## Japanese

The IJA had built a lean, infantry-heavy force configured to win an early victory by advancing quickly, penetrating or flanking when possible, and trusting the superior Japanese warrior spirit, *bushidō*, to vanquish the foe swiftly. The Japanese High Command mistakenly believed that this type of army would not be hampered by the inadequacies of Japan's industrial base, because it required neither state-of-the-art mechanization nor a cumbersome logistical tail. A reliance on material goods, necessitating an extensive supply network, was viewed by the dominating forces within the Japanese High Command as a modern evil that would destroy the fighting spirit of the IJA. Also, the IJA High Command consistently resisted weapons modernization because they feared that it would lead to an abandonment of the infantry's tradition of hand-to-hand combat to win the decisive victory.

The Japanese leadership in Burma was initially content simply to garrison the country; after all, they surmised, it was not like China, where they were combatting organized troops. The Japanese 18th Division had its three regiments initially divided for both patrolling and garrisoning. For example, one regiment was deployed to the Hukawng Valley, while another was garrisoning the Indaw area. The third regiment was stationed at 18th Division headquarters at Myitkyina. However, with the passage of time, vigorous patrolling from garrisons was to become the norm for the Japanese occupiers of Burma. For example, the activities of British-led Kachin insurgents necessitated vigorous patrolling by the Japanese in the area north of Myitkyina and not merely garrisoning the town and waiting for an attack. The effects upon the Japanese of the Kachins' guerrilla activities should not be discounted in any assessment of the effectiveness of the Chindit operations. Attacked by the IJA's 114th Infantry Regiment (18th Division), Sumprabum lay between Fort Hertz, the last British bastion in northern Burma, to the north and Myitkyina to the south.

According to Private Fujino Hideo of the 114th Infantry Regiment, who was finally to see some action against the enemy, 'At last, February in 1943, a combat broke out against the enemy at Sumprabum … the punitive force formed of the elements of the 2nd Infantry Bn of the 114th Regiment' (Fujino 1964: i). Clearly, it would not be the entire 18th Division that would be devoting its resources and manpower to defending northern Burma against the Chindit incursion, as the Kachins would inflict many casualties on the men of the 114th Infantry Regiment. Fujino stated after the war:

> Our enemy was not actually British, Chinese, nor Indians but the Kachins. They were quicker than monkeys and talented in shooting … After the eight month occupation, the punitive force at Sumprabum [132 miles to the north of Myitkyina] suffered heavy damage and the casualties from the Kachins' guerrilla tactics … In the course of the campaign, the killed and wounded amounted to a great number. For example, the commander of the 2nd Battalion was seriously wounded and the commander of the Heavy Machine Gun Company was killed in action. (Fujino 1964: ii)

The Japanese did not just sit back and wait to be attacked. In the Hukawng Valley and the Indaw area, the garrisons were really, in effect, forward outposts. The vastness of the jungle, however, meant that each Japanese infantry battalion always had to be split up into smaller units for active patrolling. The division of Japanese battalions into smaller *ad hoc* units meant that time and again during both *Longcloth* and *Thursday*, the men of 18th Division would mount attacks against the British in a piecemeal fashion without an overwhelming concentration of force.

Japanese infantry marching in full kit through thick vegetation. The seeming ease with which these troops could overcome nature's adversities was, in part, related to their extensive conditioning marches as conscripts. The Japanese infantrymen also received an abundance of instructional pamphlets that were laboriously compiled by Colonel Tsuji Masanobu, who headed up a research centre on the island of Formosa which strove to educate the soldiers about requisite jungle tactics and conditions before 18th Division invaded Malaya and Singapore as part of 25th Army (Lieutenant-General Yamashita Tomoyoki). Up until that time, 18th Division had served in China in climate and terrain vastly different from those of Malaya and Burma. Japanese rifle companies in Burma, by virtue of the geographic extent of their patrolling, acted more as independent units. These patrols were always smaller in size than the usual Chindit column of 400 men. Furthermore, the aggressive doctrine drummed into the Japanese infantry frequently led them into hasty action against numerically superior enemy forces rather than waiting for a concentration of force to defeat the British decisively. (USAMHI)

# LEADERSHIP, WEAPONS AND TACTICS

Wingate's new USAAF (United States Army Air Force) allies were colonels John Alison (left) and Philip Cochran (right), pictured here with Wingate. This triumvirate revolutionized LRP operations with a myriad of aircraft and creative tactics. Wingate's new doctrine for Operation *Thursday* was dependent on his newly formed alliance with 1st Air Commando Group, under the control of Cochran and Alison. The 1st Air Commando Group would furnish all the transport as well as parachute resupply, in addition to providing 'aerial artillery' for Wingate's brigades. This novel aerial dimension allowed Wingate to exist behind enemy lines without any land or sea LOC. Wingate's air component would revolutionize LRP as the heavy machine guns, cannon and bombs carried by fighter-bombers (P-47 Thunderbolts, P-51 Mustangs, and RAF Spitfires and Vengeances) and medium bombers (B-25 Mitchells) became aerial artillery for close infantry support. The transports (C-46 Commando and C-47 Dakota), 100 Stinson L-5 Sentinel liaison aircraft and over 200 Waco gliders would provide supplies, armaments, reinforcements and casualty evacuation with precision, enabled by state-of-the-art radio communications. In a meeting with Wingate, Cochran assured him that the Chindits had only to 'dream up' ideas and he would put them into operation. (NARA RG-208-PU-223 N-1)

Wingate bordered on the martinet and required his senior and junior officers not only to obey orders, but to espouse his doctrine when communicating with their own NCOs and men. He expected that as circumstances dictated, his junior officers would display initiative by interpreting his sometimes cryptic, biblically focused directives and turn them into action plans. The Japanese, though, never had such a change in tactical doctrine. Their tactical focus was always on the attack, and junior officers did not veer from this approach. It is fair to say that the jungle environment, in any situation, had the potential to introduce chaos into plans, often causing many casualties or the ruin of smaller formations.

There were very few weapons in use by either side that were designed for jungle warfare; however, many could not be used because of the terrain and the tactical nature of the mission undertaken by both sides. The Japanese employed only lighter, lower-calibre artillery in Burma; the Chindits had no artillery at all for *Longcloth*, but developed 'aerial artillery', delivered by 1st Air Commando Group, as a new tactical model for *Thursday*. At the individual level, a high degree of marksmanship was desirable since the terrain would often allow only a transient glimpse of the enemy and conservation of ammunition was paramount given the logistical difficulties faced by both sides. The nature of the jungle terrain often meant the two sides clashed in impromptu, spontaneous engagements, or in prepared ambushes; these often resulted in hand-to-hand combat, meaning close-quarter combat skills and appropriate weaponry were particularly important.

## British

Wingate's leadership of the Chindits or Special Force was a novel enterprise:

> Stilwell, an American officer, had the great advantage of working from a fixed military doctrine covering strategy and tactics … In Special Force things were very different. Wingate had to reduce guerrilla tactics to a system and then, partly from his experience and partly from his enormously inventive imagination, produce 'drills', or 'standard operating procedures' for marching in jungle, blowing up bridges, bivouacking, crossing river, crossing open spaces, receiving a supply drop from the air, laying an ambush, attacking a village, taking evasive action in jungle and, in extreme danger, dispersing into small parties to re-assemble in an area some distance away. He wrote or drafted all the more important instructions himself. At the same time, his thoughts began to move more and more to alternating guerrilla tactics with conventional attack and defence. (Bidwell 1979: 51)

During *Longcloth*, a tremendous amount of operational latitude was given to the commanders of the columns and smaller units. After all, the tactic of dispersal and rendezvous, if it were to be successful, had to be put into practice at the group and individual levels. However, for some columns, especially in Southern Group during *Longcloth*, the tactic of dispersal and rendezvous would result in profound confusion due to the previously untested leadership skills of some junior officers. On two occasions during *Longcloth*, columns were entirely lost after dispersal, thereby disappearing from the Chindit order

An RAF Vultee A-31 Vengeance returns to Assam after a dive-bombing sortie in close support of Chindit infantrymen against Japanese troops in the Burmese jungle in the spring of 1944. This American-built aircraft was a two-seater dive-bomber and attack warplane with a range of 1,400 miles. Its armament was impressive as an infantry-support weapon, including six .50-calibre fixed forward-firing machine guns in the leading edges of the wings. The plane also had a rearward-firing .50-calibre machine gun in the rear cockpit for defence against IJA fighters, such as the very capable Ki-43 *Hayabusa* or 'Oscar'. In order to attack IJA troop concentrations the A-31 had an external load of two 500lb bombs, which can be seen on the bomb ammunition trailer in the foreground. The aircraft of 1st Air Commando Group would become Wingate's 'flying artillery'. (NARA RG-208-AA-11B-2)

of battle. Even so, during *Longcloth* Wingate was able to direct most of his columns via wireless and executed another of his tactics; namely, the feint, where he would send one column toward the Japanese to enable other columns to slip through the gaps in the IJA patrols. The best example of this involved Maj Scott's No. 8 Column demonstrating on Pinbon, while Calvert's No. 3 Column and Maj Bernard Fergusson's No. 5 Column were able to arrive at the railway undetected to begin their demolition work. Wingate did attempt to co-ordinate the remaining columns' movement to cross and re-cross the Irrawaddy, but by the end of March 1943 it was apparent that only small units would be able to evade the tightening Japanese noose. So, although the Chindit junior officers were allowed tremendous initiative and independence during their retreat, the nature of the withdrawal – along with terrain obstacles (mostly rivers) – often resulted in a chaotic trek.

There was a tactical paradigm shift for *Thursday*; Wingate and his officers now wanted to lure the Japanese to attack their 'strongholds' and blocks to inflict maximum casualties with their heavier weapons that were not present during *Longcloth*. Lt-Gen Slim did offer to furnish the Chindit garrisons with a number of 25-pdr field-artillery pieces and Bofors 40mm anti-aircraft guns for defence against enemy infantry, artillery and air attack – an offer Wingate accepted. Wingate believed that light artillery was useful for keeping the enemy's heads down, but unlikely to kill, so he did not have any with his columns in either operation. With Wingate's 'strongholds' having airstrips for light liaison and heavier C-47 transport aircraft, the wounded would no longer have to be left behind, in contrast to Operation *Longcloth* in 1943. This fact was an immediate boost to morale.

For Operation *Longcloth*, the Chindits had been instructed to practise evasion techniques in a firefight. Wingate defined 'mobility' as 'the power a column possesses to move away from an enemy in such a way and into such country that the enemy will be unable or afraid to follow it and how pursuit should be discouraged by the setting of booby traps by the rearguard on the

# COMBAT

## Superior private, I/55th Infantry

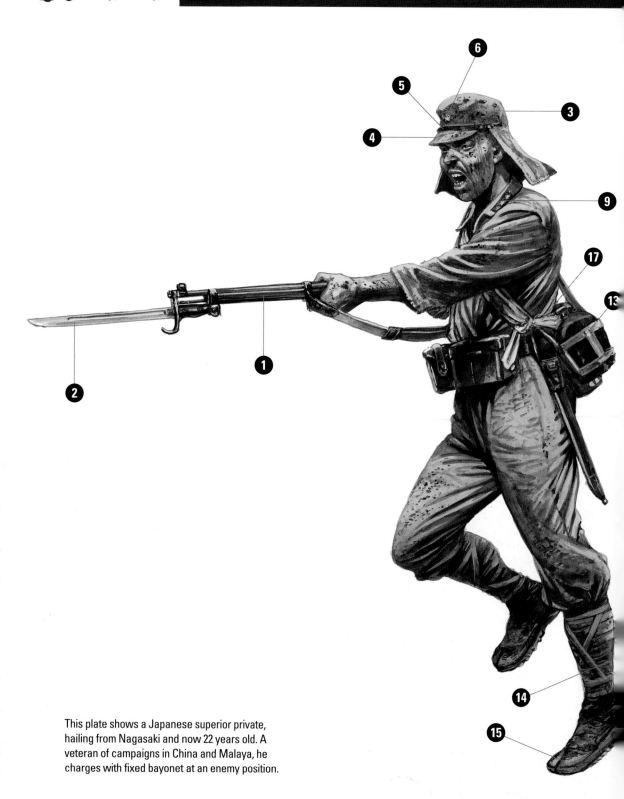

This plate shows a Japanese superior private, hailing from Nagasaki and now 22 years old. A veteran of campaigns in China and Malaya, he charges with fixed bayonet at an enemy position.

## Weapons, dress and equipment

This soldier is armed with the 7.7mm Type 99 Arisaka bolt-action rifle (**1**). It was 6in shorter than the older Meiji Type 38 rifle that used a 6.5mm round, making the Type 99 more suitable for the fighting amid jungle vegetation. His rifle weighs 8.16lb with a length of 44.1in. The weapon had a five-round internal magazine and an effective range of just over 545yd. Attached to the rifle is a Type 30 sword bayonet (**2**), which weighed 16.6oz and had an overall length of 20.1in (blade length 15.7in) and a width of 0.75in. The bayonet was fixed over the muzzle and had a hooked quillon and a curved pommel.

Since he hastily deployed from his truck after an anti-tank round detonated in it, this infantryman lacks his helmet. He wears the Japanese field cap made of cloth (**3**). The cap had a short stiffened peak (**4**) in the same material, which was sharply angled downwards, and a brown leather chinstrap (**5**). A small star on a circular cloth backing (**6**) was positioned on the front vertical seam of the cap and was gold in colour for enlisted men. Here, the field cap is worn with four separate lowered neck flaps (**7**) for sun protection in tropical climes; there were prominent ventilation holes (**8**) around the crown of the cap. He wears the red collar badges of a superior private with three five-point gold stars (**9**) on his lightweight tropical shirt (**10**), which is tucked into his tropical-weight trousers.

Leather ammunition pouches containing 7.7mm cartridges are worn on the front of the belt: one on each side, and a third on the back of the belt (**11**). The haversack or *zatsumo* (**12**) was carried at all times and was made of a heavy cotton or rayon canvas with a single compartment to carry rations, a spare sock with rice, and personal items. It was slung over the shoulder with a wide strap. A small metal hook allowed the attachment of the haversack to the belt to lighten its weight and prevent it from swinging. A water bottle (**13**) is slung over the right shoulder and rests on the left hip. Cloth puttees (**14**) give protection and support to the lower legs and are held in place by cotton tapes, which were often tied off in a cross pattern over the front. The distinctive split-toe sole of the lightweight *Tabi* boot (**15**) gave better grip on difficult terrain or when climbing walls or trees. The metal bayonet scabbard with leather belt attachment (**16**) hangs down over his left hip and upper leg. A *senninbari* ('sash of the one thousand stitches', (**17**) made of cotton or rayon and inscribed with best wishes is worn across the chest by this infantryman to impress his fellow Japanese soldiers and their enemies. Altogether, this soldier's combat load weighs about 30lb.

tracks of the column' (quoted in Bidwell 1979: 51). The preparation for *Thursday* posed some problems, since new senior and junior officers were being brought into the Chindits from the veteran 70th Division; these newcomers would have to learn Wingate's doctrine, while his cadres from *Longcloth* were already 'disciples'. Also, while new Chindits were being trained for *Thursday*, Wingate's doctrine was evolving towards more aggressive action. This was never sufficiently impressed on the units training for *Thursday*, since Wingate was in hospital for a long time suffering from typhoid fever. For both *Longcloth* and *Thursday* the Lee-Enfield rifle, Thompson submachine gun, Bren gun, Boys anti-tank rifle, Vickers medium machine gun, and 2in and 3in mortars were among the usual infantry weapons utilized by Wingate's force. Occasionally, PIAT hand-held anti-tank weapons and flamethrowers would be used against Japanese entrenched pillboxes, again notably at Mogaung. Short-range weapons such as the Thompson submachine gun and the hand grenade were most valued for jungle fighting at short distances. Whereas in Europe artillery and automatic fire dominated the battlefield, in Burma marksmanship mattered. An unaimed bullet was likely to damage only vegetation.

## Japanese

The officer corps of the IJA consisted of regular and reserve officers. A high percentage of IJA officers during World War II were graduates of the reserve officer training programme. After completion of their training, both regular and reserve officers served as probationary officers in their units for two to six months. While infantrymen perfected their bayonet drills, officers practised with swords alongside them, demonstrating to the men that their officers were at least as tough and well trained in hand-to-hand combat as the soldiers were. In the field, officers prided themselves on sharing the same hardships as their men. Japanese NCOs came from three sources in the IJA: technical branch youth apprentice schools; the reserve officer candidate system; and promotion from the ranks. As in most armies of the era, NCOs lived with their troops and were responsible for lower-level individual and collective training. For the

Japanese infantry get ready for a bayonet charge. In combat, Japanese infantry strove to outflank their enemy and either close with them with the bayonet or set up a roadblock in their rear. Both tactics instilled terror into a demoralized opponent. Here, one soldier's bayonet has a white cloth suspended from the bayonet called a *senninbari* or 'sash of one thousand stitches'. It was made of cotton or rayon and was folded along the edges and sported leather triangles at the corners to hold the cords. The *senninbari* would be worn about the waist, chest, or, as here, attached to the infantryman's rifle. The *senninbari* was inscribed with best wishes, poems and good-luck phrases by family, workmates or fellow soldiers. (USAMHI)

Japanese, initiative among junior officers and NCOs was not the norm. Instead, strict obedience to orders without deviation was the rule, often leading to catastrophic effects during attacks on well-entrenched and -supplied Chindit forces, notably at the 'strongholds'.

In 1942–43 the Japanese soldier had proved to be a master at incorporating the terrain as an added combat dimension. Although the Japanese infantryman was well conditioned for the arduous forced marches and was

excellent in hand-to-hand combat, in terms of his equipment, he was by no means a 'superman'. Early in 1942, the Japanese infantryman wore the same uniform used in China's more temperate, and even colder, climate. As tropical-weight uniforms were developed – though these were not always available to front-line troops – the Japanese infantryman's individual clothing and equipment became better suited to a fast-moving, mobile campaign in the tropics. The usual load of an IJA infantryman was a steel helmet, a belt with at least one ammunition pouch, a bayonet, a light pack and an entrenching tool. Most soldiers had a camouflage net, several feet long, that they could drape over themselves and stuff with foliage to make themselves less visible in the jungle.

The principal tactic for the Japanese infantryman was to close with the enemy, often by surprise during the hours of darkness, and combat his adversary with the cold steel of the bayonet. Japanese doctrine stressed that the bayonet was the soldier's most essential weapon. With a blade 15.7in long, the bayonet was almost always fixed rather than carried, as its weight helped to balance the rifle. Both light machine guns (LMGs) and heavy machine guns (HMGs) were utilized by the Japanese infantrymen at ambush sites. The Type 11 6.5mm LMG was a poor weapon and remained in service only because it was relatively easy to manufacture. The Type 96 LMG was a better gun; based on the Czech ZB vz. 26 design, it had a 30-round box magazine attached to the top of the gun. It was 2.5lb lighter, weighing 20lb. Even IJA machine-gunners attached bayonets to their squad LMGs. The infantry battalion also had separate HMG companies, each fielding 8–12 Type 92 HMGs. Crewed by up to eight men, this gun fired a heavier 7.7mm bullet and when mounted on its tripod, weighed 122lb.

For the IJA, artillery's sole role was to support the infantry, thus, the guns were light-weight, thereby sacrificing both range and ruggedness against Allied artillery. In keeping with the IJA's mobile offensive doctrine, commanders pushed artillery all the way down to the battalion level. The battalion gun platoon was equipped with two Type 92 7cm battalion guns with an effective range of 1,500yd and a maximum range of 3,000yd; these were often employed in a direct-fire role. Unlike comparable Allied guns, the Type 92 could be broken down and carried by its ten-man gun section.

A two-man Japanese infantry team load and fire a 5cm Type 89 grenade discharger, which was the IJA's most widespread fire-support weapon for the infantry; each platoon carried three. The discharger weighed 10.4lb and could fire high explosive (HE), smoke, incendiary or signal rounds. Allied soldiers misnamed this weapon a 'knee mortar'. Although it could fire signal and smoke shells, this grenade discharger was primarily used with the infantry's standard 19oz Type 91 hand grenade, which had a maximum range of 175yd, in contrast to this same hand grenade being able to be lobbed to about 75yd at most. When the Type 89 shell was used, a range of 730yd could be reached by adjusting the position of the trigger housing within the leg of the weapon, thus changing the position of the firing pin within the barrel and lengthening the trajectory of the shell. This weapon inflicted an incredibly high percentage of casualties among Allied infantrymen and could be used much more easily in the jungle by the Japanese than traditional mortars. That said, 7cm and 8.1cm mortars were also utilized. (USAMHI)

Because of its versatility and mobility, the battalion gun was present in most infantry engagements. The regimental gun company fielded four 75mm Type 38 regimental guns, but because it required either six horses or 13 men to pull it, the Type 38 was not suitable for combat in the Burmese jungle. As with artillery, the tank's main role was believed to be infantry support. Japanese infantry divisions received small quantities of the Type 94 'tankette', which was essentially a gun carrier lighter than 4 tons. It had a crew of two and a 6.5mm machine gun. Its 12mm-thick armour made it susceptible to Allied small-arms and anti-tank fire.

## COMMUNICATIONS, LOGISTICS AND MORALE

Communication was problematic for both sides fighting in Burma, because portable radios seldom worked. Even at very close range, the close terrain often made it hard to see hand signals from officers or NCOs. In terms of logistics, it was apparent that an absence of motor transport forced British and Japanese alike to rely heavily on pack animals for transporting supplies. Both sides also had to learn pertinent medical treatments, both for themselves and for their animals. Separate detachments in both forces stressed the need for water purification as a means of lessening the risks posed by cholera and dysentery, as well as anti-malarial prophylaxis and prevention.

Although the determination to succeed in the conflict remained, one can sense a despondency among the average soldier. The Japanese referred to the Hukawng Valley as the 'Valley of Death' not out of fear of Stilwell's Sino-American troops but rather the harsh terrain and pestilence that characterized that setting. For the Chindits, Wingate's leadership helped to motivate the average soldier during the early days of *Longcloth*; however, hunger, natural hardships and the abandonment of the wounded soon became demoralizing. For the average Japanese and British participants in the Burma campaign,

their understanding of their role was at the sectional level and centred principally upon survival – in sharp contrast to the high command, consumed with achieving the tactical and strategic aims of the mission.

Both the British Chindit and the IJA infantryman knew that once on the line, there would be no chance of returning to rear-echelon areas unless severely wounded or deathly ill. This was due to a need to keep the ranks full and the paucity or absence of motor transport. In fact, for the Chindit during *Longcloth*, no such rear-echelon areas existed. With the advent of light aircraft

Japanese troops emerging from the jungle with each infantryman carrying a component of a disassembled field artillery piece. The Japanese infantry would often use the jungle to get behind their enemy and by so doing set up an attacking position in their rear. The ability to get off the motor road, trail or jungle track and use the verdant foliage to conceal flanking movements around the enemy had become the norm and was a winning tactic over the road-bound Allied soldier, in addition to instilling an air of panic or rout – especially in the British and Indian troops in Burma in 1942, since these retreating troops had been outflanked by infiltration through jungle deemed impassable. These enveloping tactics caused considerable disorder among the Allied soldiers, who now found themselves combatting the Japanese in both directions, often with pressure being exerted on their flanks as well. Note that one of the soldiers is carrying the *hinomaru*, or 'flag of the rising sun', derogatorily called 'meatball' by the Allies, which was often given to a soldier by his family to keep his spirits high. (USAMHI)

to evacuate wounded, the rear areas during *Thursday* became hospitals in Assam. Interestingly, when Lt Archie Wavell, the Viceroy's son, was wounded at Mogaung while serving in Calvert's 77th Indian Infantry Brigade, he dutifully waited his turn for air evacuation – much to the consternation of Wingate's replacement, Maj-Gen Lentaigne, who had been exerting pressure to get him out sooner because of political ramifications.

## British

Wingate had to ensure that contact between his Chindits and RAF bases and airborne supply transports was always maintained, through his RAF signallers. Three types of standard radios were used in the field during Operations *Longcloth* and *Thursday*, to provide adequate communication at various levels of the battle order. First, communication within the column utilized a Wireless Set (WS) No. 19 – often made into a WS No. 19 HP (High Power), giving it considerably greater range – which required a mule for transport. This was the only available set for the typical 15-mile range. The second type of radio set, the WS No. 22, enabled columns to communicate with brigade HQ, 30–60 miles away, and was a very durable device. A third variety of radio set was used for communications between HQ and Corps HQ, often over long distances, and required relay stations situated at higher elevations; it too needed pack-animal transport due to its weight.

Each Chindit carried a pack weighing about 60lb, while pack mules carried additional supplies. Many Chindits wore beards, making carrying a shaving kit unnecessary, and also helping to protect the facial skin from mosquitoes and ticks. Rations were less than 2lb per day, consisting of biscuits, cheese, nuts, raisins, dates, tea, sugar, milk and chocolate. This ration supplied approximately 3,000 calories, which was insufficient. These rations were sometimes supplemented by rice, bananas and other fruit from friendly villagers to acquire an additional 1,000 calories, which were needed for troops in the field marching 20–25 miles each day. Some supplies were dropped by

A C-47 Dakota parachutes supplies into a pre-arranged drop zone as Chindits await their arrival. Static lines tripped the parachutes to open once out of the transport's cabin. These aircraft often flew their supply missions without any fighter cover and were always prone to attack by the Imperial Japanese Army's Ki-43 *Hayabusa* 'Oscar' fighters. Some supplies such as animal feed or fruit was free-dropped without parachutes, with one of the dangers of this approach being injury to Chindits on the ground being struck by the heavy parcel. The Dakota transport aircraft was utilized by both the USAAF and the RAF to resupply the Chindits during the Burmese missions where they had no land-based LOC. To make their drops, these aircraft flew over hazardous mountainous terrain behind enemy lines. On rare occasions during Operation *Longcloth*, a C-47 Dakota would land at an emergency airstrip to evacuate some wounded Chindits. During Operation *Thursday*, it would be the C-47s that would tow the Waco gliders to the Chindit landing zones. (USAMHI)

Stinson L-5 Sentinel liaison aircraft taxi onto an airstrip at White City to evacuate the wounded from the railway block at Henu during Operation *Thursday*. Wingate made it clear to his Chindits that his columns would not stop and wait for sick or wounded stragglers. They would be left to the care of Burmese villagers and, more often, the pursuing Japanese. During and after Operation *Longcloth*, the abandonment of the seriously wounded led to a deterioration of morale within the Chindit ranks and criticism of Wingate's methods. This contentious tenet was addressed by Wingate for Operation *Thursday* by having 1st Air Commando Group evacuate wounded Chindits from rudimentary airstrips using Stinson L-5 Sentinel liaison aircraft, or from the larger 'stronghold' airfields via C-47 Dakota aircraft. (NARA 208-AA-11B-14)

air, but this became more difficult when the columns had to disperse. Some British soldiers found themselves receiving special training as mule handlers, and many grew fond of their charges. All ranks had to be carefully instructed in packing saddles, for overloading caused girth sores, or worse. Four mules designated for a rifle-company HQ, for instance, could carry 158lb apiece. Mortars and Vickers guns were dismantled for mule portage. Chindit officers were issued with horses, which rather than riding, most used to carry personal effects such as blankets, a mosquito net or a rifle in a saddle bucket. When supplies were air-dropped, these included corn in vast quantities for the pack train. Beyond mules, Japanese and British alike exploited elephants. The animals, each with their *oozie* – an indigenous elephant-handler – had been employed before the war in Burma's teak forests. Although, surprisingly, each elephant could carry little more than a mule's load, their bridge-building skills were much in demand. Some 4,000 elephants are estimated to have died in Burma between 1942 and 1945.

Lt R. Allen Wilding, originally posted to 6th Gurkha Rifles in India and working as a ciphers officer, stated, 'He [Wingate] never threw a life away, but you always felt that he realized that his life and the life of each of us was expendable if it was necessary' (quoted in Thompson 2003: 65). Wingate believed every infantryman needed to be his own medic, so along with his other indoctrination lectures and demonstrations, ample time was spent on rudimentary medical care. There were medics and some physicians present with the Chindit forces during the operations in Burma, but the horror of having to leave wounded behind during *Longcloth* was so unnerving that Wingate made major tactical changes for *Thursday*, with the construction of airstrips to evacuate those seriously wounded by light aircraft, as well as more substantial airstrips capable of accommodating Dakota transports to ferry out the wounded after having brought in air-landed supplies and reinforcements to the 'strongholds'.

## Japanese

The Japanese infantryman, like his civilian counterpart, was torn between two principles: *giri*, an obligation to the community, and *ninjō*, personal responsibility. Membership in the Japanese community was perceived as a chain derived from the nucleus of the state, the Emperor. Defying this tradition was regarded as a lack of integrity rather than as independent thinking, while distancing oneself from the Emperor was viewed as a personal tragedy and family shame. This combination of obedience to the Emperor and one's moral essence helps to explain some of the strict adherence to orders and warrior code, *bushidō*, as well as the refusal to disgrace oneself and family by surrendering as a soldier. The Japanese soldier was well known for his disregard for death. *Bushidō* contributed significantly to a soldier's supreme sacrifice, which demonstrated the qualities of honour, courage and moral purity. As an extension to the warrior code, soldiers believed in their innate superiority and their sacred mission of subjugating any foe in the name of the Emperor. In order to deter individualism or exhibition of initiative, *Seishin kyōiku* or spiritual training was imposed at all levels of the army to foster blind submission to the Emperor.

The Japanese infantryman was instructed in sanitation, personal hygiene and first aid, but dedicated detachments for disease prevention and water purification were needed to try to minimize outbreaks of cholera and malaria. However, indoctrinated into the IJA infantryman's credo was that although prepared physically, psychologically, and spiritually for combat,

A Japanese signals soldier operates his wireless system's Morse key in the jungle. Wire communications were the preferred mode in the jungle for their reliability, but the laying of telephone wire in this terrain was extremely difficult. Also, the use of field telephones was relegated almost exclusively to situations where a position was completely secured. The wireless radio equipment was of high quality, but it soon became obsolete by the standards of Western armies. The intense jungle humidity rusted and destroyed many of the internal components of the radios. Also, if mountainous terrain was present, decreased efficiency occurred. The lack of standardization produced a major supply problem for the IJA, amplified by the difficulty in delivering these devices and their components to remote jungle locales. Thus, commanders often had to rely on messengers, thereby limiting a centralization of orders during fast-moving offensives. (USAMHI)

The inadequate transport system of the IJA forced soldiers to use all types of improvised methods to carry heavy loads of equipment during long marches or over difficult terrain, such as Burmese mountains and rivers. The most common mode of transportation was the march, often causing the soles of the infantryman's shoes to wear out soon after the Burmese invasion. Although the IJA utilized horses, mules and elephants as pack animals, here Japanese infantrymen are carrying artillery shells in addition to their own heavy kit and personal gear. The ammunition cylinders are carried in wooden harnesses attached to the backs of the infantrymen, with ropes securing the shells. According to Private Hirai Saukichi, an infantryman in III/114th Infantry (18th Division), 'Once in Burma, supplies for extra ammunition becomes more and more heavy. Food is scarce, I couldn't stretch my week rice ration beyond eight days and I now can't count but on two emergency pieces of biscuit. Men and beasts suffer from the marching in the jungle, and going through immense valleys and cliffs ... each of us is given a 75 mm artillery shell which is fitted inside the knapsack next to the scarce, almost nonexistent food ...' (quoted in Sáiz 2011: 22). (USAMHI)

the possibility of being wounded was not even considered. Failure to give the last drop of blood for the Emperor was dishonourable, as was being convalescent without justification. In sum, the medical corps of the IJA was inadequate to provide the necessary care to any army the size of the Japanese armed forces during World War II. Despite the dehumanizing effects of his training, the Japanese infantryman in Burma would often keep the ashes of his fallen comrades in boxes and try to heal the wounded as best his limited medical supplies would allow.

The most important thing was to keep the soldier's inner spirit high, avoiding any weakness and assuring unconditional loyalty to the Emperor. The external appearances were secondary and often considered mundane and superfluous. However, with the reversal of fortunes for the 18th Division infantryman by the late spring of 1944 in northern Burma, the stresses caused by the paucity of food and inability to wash due to a shortage of water contributed to a breakdown in morale. Owing to the Chindits' interdiction of the north–south railway and motor road at Henu during Operation *Thursday* in 1944, Private Fujino Hideo of II/114th Infantry noted, there was

an extreme lack of ammunition and food [as well as] battle casualties and other losses on our side amount to much ... Even a wounded soldier with one arm and one leg had to fight with a gun and hand grenades. It was only the high morale among men and the perfect unity of the whole army that made us cling so stubbornly. (Fujino 1964: iii)

# Nankan Station

## 6 March 1943

## BACKGROUND TO BATTLE

On the night of 13/14 February 1943, Operation *Longcloth* began with the crossing of the Chindwin River. Wingate's main body (Northern Group) – comprised of Nos 3, 4, 5, 7 and 8 columns – crossed the Chindwin at Tonhe, where the river is only 400yd wide. The entire Northern Group had crossed the Chindwin by 18 February. Lt-Col Hugh T. Alexander's Southern Group (Nos 1 and 2 columns), acting as a diversionary force to draw attention away from the main effort in the north, had crossed the Chindwin 50 miles to the south, near Auktaung, by the early morning of 16 February.

The Chindits' first encounter with the enemy occurred when elements of Southern Group clashed with a small Japanese force at Maingnyaung on 18 February. Southern Group believed there was a Japanese garrison of 250 men at Maingnyaung and proceeded to set an ambush for them. However, the combat situation deteriorated. Three Gurkha platoons met an enemy patrol that afternoon. Gunfire erupted and six Japanese soldiers were killed. The Japanese retreated and after alerting their headquarters about the skirmish, the Gurkhas were bombarded with Japanese mortar bombs. The Gurkha transport officer sent the animals to the rear; however, the muleteers panicked and ran back to the Chindwin River, stampeding many of their animals in the process. A substantial number of the mules were missing for several days while many others were never found, thereby reducing supplies and removing the element of a surprise attack on the Japanese garrison.

On 2 March, Southern Group's No. 2 Column was bivouacking in the Wild Life Sanctuary Forest a couple of miles west of the railway station at Kyaikthin in anticipation of the next day's attack to blow it up when it was ambushed by a full Japanese battalion (see the Introduction). No. 2 Column was forced to disperse and head back to India as it lacked signal equipment, medical stores or reserve ammunition and could not contact Wingate to arrange for an air drop. Thus, No. 2 Column ceased to exist as part of Wingate's order of battle; however, in the process it acted as the requisite diversionary force and drew hundreds of Japanese towards it and away from Northern Group. According to Lance Corporal Shinsaku Honma of the 2nd Machine Gun Company, 215th Infantry Regiment:

While we had been enjoying a peaceful occupation in Monywa, we were told that a British force had penetrated into Burma, and our 2nd Battalion had arrived at Kanbalu railway station (about 100 kilometres south-east of Pinlebu) from Monywa on 28 February 1943 … In order to trap the enemy ten men, including myself from the Machine Gun Company, were attached to 7th Rifle Company and advanced towards the Yu River.

We arrived at the village as ordered but we found no signs of the enemy … When we woke the next morning there were no … village people [present] … At about [1000hrs] I was roused by the sentry's alarm. Again seven or eight enemy soldiers [Chindits] came walking leisurely with rifles on shoulder straps. I knew that I should not let them escape into the jungle again ... I aimed exactly at the waist of the man in front, so that even if he lay flat the bullets would hit the men in the rear … [I] pressed the trigger … the leading three men fell down one by one. Then I moved my aim to the remaining men who lay flat and fired another thirty bullets; 7th [Rifle] Company ran to the enemy and found two men killed and five wounded. I was impressed by the excellent performance of the Type 92 medium machine gun. (Quoted in Nunneley & Tamayama 2000: 116–19)

Several days later, L/Cpl George Bell, a section commander in 13th King's, was with Wingate's Northern Group HQ. He later recalled:

> We then crossed the Zibyu Taungdan Range by a little known path which had been used by British troops and civilians the previous year, during the retreat to India. Quite a few skeletons at the side of the track of those who did not make it. Occasionally met lads of other columns who had had several skirmishes with the Japs. The position at that time was one of aggression in that orders were given to attack Japs wherever possible or feasible. (Quoted in Chinnery 2010: 56)

Led by Colonel Koba Hiroshi, the Japanese 55th Infantry Regiment (18th Division) was responsible for the area west of the Zibyu Range, roughly from Homalin to Mawlaik. The northern part of this area was the responsibility of I/55th Infantry, with the Regimental HQ and half of I/55th Infantry at Katha on the Irrawaddy River. Probably by coincidence rather than actual planning, 77th Indian Infantry Brigade would advance through the operational boundary between 18th and 33rd divisions. The first sighting of the Chindit incursion was made by Major Shigemi Nagano, commanding I/55th Infantry. On 17 February he signalled to Koba, 'According to local reports, enemy about three to four thousand strong on a march eastward from area Paungbyin' (quoted in Allen 2000: 133). Although initially sceptical about this intelligence, after he reported the observation to Mutaguchi, Koba ordered I/55th Infantry and III/55th Infantry to find and destroy the Chindit force as he moved his own headquarters from Katha westwards towards Indaw with half of I/55th Infantry under his command. Mutaguchi did not think at the time that the Chindit force was much of a threat and left the search-and-destroy mission in Koba's hands. At the time, the Japanese did not know that the Chindits were being supplied by air drops and that there were no ground LOC to sever.

On 1 March, Northern Group descended into the Chaunggyi Valley not far from Pinbon. Wingate ordered Nos 4, 7 and 8 columns to manoeuvre as a feint while he sent Nos 3 and 5 columns towards the railway, tasked with demolishing it. On 4 March, No. 4 Column was ambushed south-west of Pinbon and was ordered to disperse; unable to rejoin Nos 7 and 8 columns, No. 4 Column withdrew to India. On 4–6 March, Nos 7 and 8 columns demonstrated near Pinlebu, thereby confusing the Japanese as to Wingate's intentions. Owing to the Japanese infantry's offensive-mindedness at this stage of the Burmese conflict, elements of 18th and 33rd divisions were rushed from the area of the railway towards the Chindit 'feint' to counter the threat on Pinlebu in the Mu Valley, thereby allowing Maj Michael Calvert's No. 3 Column and Maj Bernard Fergusson's No. 5 Column to 'thrust' unhindered towards their next strategic location, the Wuntho–Indaw section of the Burmese railway, which ran north–south from Myitkyina to Mandalay.

Japanese infantry skirmish with Chindits in dense jungle during Operation *Longcloth*. Wingate sought to indoctrinate the Chindits about the utilization of the jungle's overgrowth for concealment from the more numerous Japanese. Dense jungle would also offer safety with his rapid dispersal and rendezvous tactic when attacked by a larger enemy force. At the battle of Nankan Station, Calvert's ambush parties, although partially concealed, did not disperse when Japanese lorried infantry approached them down the motor road from Indaw. Instead, they tried to hold their ground while the demolition parties did their task. The signals party with the mules, however, did disperse to the pre-arranged jungle rendezvous point. (USAMHI)

**MAP KEY**

**1 1245hrs:** Having rested with the remainder of Maj Calvert's No. 3 Column in a secure bivouac since the evening of 4 March, the demolition crews of No. 1 Party move onto the railway, 3 miles south-west of Nankan Station, and start laying charges on the line as they go.

**2 1245hrs:** No. 2 Party's demolition crews move onto the railway 3 miles north of Nankan Station to set explosives.

**3 1315hrs:** Two truckloads of Japanese troops from I/55th Infantry plus a light tank race down the road from Indaw to the north and drive right into No. 4 Party's ambush, just north-west of Nankan Station. The first truck is hit by a round from a Boys anti-tank rifle and six Japanese soldiers are killed. The remainder of the truckload deploys off the vehicle under Bren-gun and rifle fire. More Japanese reinforcements arrive and No. 4 Party is soon outnumbered three-to-one.

**4 1345hrs:** After Subadar Singh sends a runner to No. 6 party for assistance, Capt William Griffiths' men join No. 4 party, and send one runner to inform Calvert of the Japanese attack and another to No. 2 Party requesting another section of reinforcements from Capt George Silcock.

**5 1400hrs:** Flt Lt Thompson loads the wireless sets, which were out in the open, onto the mules and moves them across the railway into the jungle to the south where No. 3 Party has taken cover.

**6 1530hrs:** The two demolition crews' explosives, placed in 75 places at 100yd intervals along the railway line, begin to detonate in a loud series of explosions; 6 miles of railway and three bridges will be completely demolished.

**7 1600hrs:** Two small steel railway bridges, which had charges placed by the demolition crews, are demolished.

**8 1615hrs:** The larger 100ft-span steel railway bridge with its brick-topped abutments is destroyed.

**9 1615hrs:** The Japanese push back Chindits under Kum Singh and Griffiths and take control of the village of Nankan.

**10 1630hrs:** Calvert's No. 1 Party, returning toward Nankan Station from the south-west, receives machine-gun fire from a Japanese armoured vehicle. With a 60ft bridge span still to demolish, Cpl Hubert H. Day and another of Calvert's men crawl onto the bridge to lay their charges, successfully destroying it, and then seek cover on the other side.

**11 1645hrs:** Capt Erik Petersen, a Free Dane serving in the British Army, leads a party of 50 British soldiers, with some heavier weapons, down the track leading from the mountains out onto the railway; they join Calvert's party.

**12 1715hrs:** Calvert deploys to attack the enemy, first with 3in mortars and then with rifle and machine-gun fire. A second Japanese truck is destroyed by a mortar round and the Japanese who try to cross open ground to outflank the Chindits are shot down.

**13 1800hrs:** Calvert orders all parties to head swiftly south-eastwards towards the pre-arranged rendezvous, south of Tigyaing and near the Irrawaddy.

## Battlefield environment

Nankan Station was situated in a small area of completely open ground. Some 200yd to the north-west of the station was a Burmese village that was surrounded by jungle palms. A new motor road running between Indaw, 25 miles to the north, and Wuntho, 10 miles to the south, cut across the railway line just beside the station at Nankan. Surrounding the area of open ground was dense jungle on all sides. The open terrain was not ideally suited for Wingate's doctrine of ambush with subsequent dispersal. It offered a minimum of cover to conceal a Bren or Boys position; after the combat started, Calvert's ambush party's position would be evident and come under attack. Furthermore, these ambush parties had to hold their ground and not disperse. That said, the oncoming Japanese would be in plain sight on the motor road in their lorries. Another advantage for the British conferred by the open terrain in the vicinity of the ambush sites and the motor road was that Calvert was able to use his two 3in mortars without any obscuring jungle vegetation, thereby enabling his troops to place one mortar round directly into a Japanese truck. Calvert commented on the aspect of the terrain as it pertained to the end of the battle: 'At one stage a group of enemy really got the jitters and decided to chance their all in a charge. They came at us yelling their heads off but for some reason, we shall never know, they chose a spot which meant crossing open country with no cover. Every one of them died' (quoted in Bierman & Smith 1999: 279).

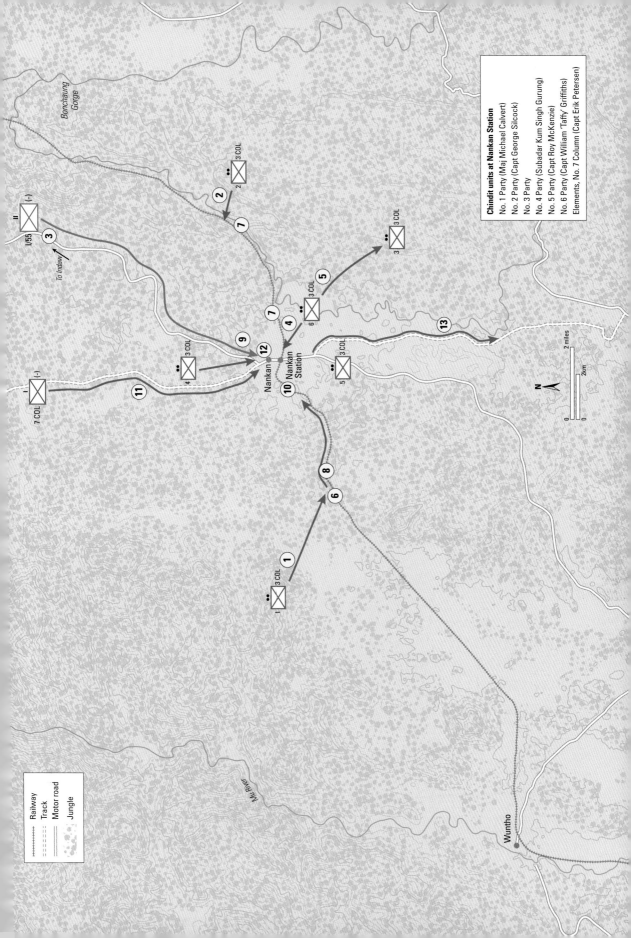

**Chindit units at Nankan Station**

No. 1 Party (Maj Michael Calvert)
No. 2 Party (Capt George Silcock)
No. 3 Party
No. 4 Party (Subadar Kum Singh Gurung)
No. 5 Party (Capt Roy McKenzie)
No. 6 Party (Capt William 'Taffy' Griffiths)
Elements, No. 7 Column (Capt Erik Petersen)

Railway
Track
Motor road
Jungle

Bonchaung Gorge

To Indaw

I/55

Nankan

Nankan Station

Mu River

Wuntho

N

2 miles
2km

3 COL
7 COL

# INTO COMBAT

When Lt Ken Gourlay's Burma Rifles reconnaissance patrol from Calvert's No. 3 Column arrived at Nankan Station on 6 March 1943, after a two-day bivouac 2 miles west of it, they found it completely deserted; however, they knew that there were 200 Japanese at Wuntho, 10 miles to the south-east, and that a motor road led straight from Wuntho through Nankan village to the station. Recalling this 48-hour interlude before the synchronized railway attack with Fergusson's No. 5 Column, Calvert stated that:

> We discovered for one thing that the Japs had not sent all their troops away to Pinlebu. As far as we could make out there were not enough left to stop us doing the job, although they might cause a bit of trouble when the bangs started and they realized we were on their doorstep. However, I was pretty confident we could hold them off without straining our resources too much ... We moved in on the 6th – my thirtieth birthday – as planned. (Calvert 1965: 133)

Although everything looked very quiet in the station, there was much evidence of the great rout and retreat of Britain's forces the previous year: scattered magazine pouches and smashed equipment; a rusted jeep; bullet-ridden trucks; a demolished locomotive lying on its side. Local villagers came to look at the Chindits and started talking with the soldiers of the Burma Rifles about recent train movements.

Calvert's No. 3 Column arrived at Nankan Station tasked with destroying the railway at as many places as possible. Calvert personally led No. 1 Party, a section-strength demolition crew, along the railway line as far as 3 miles south of Nankan Station. Capt George Silcock led another demolition crew, No. 2 Party, along the railway line as far as 3 miles north. Calvert had ordered

Maj Michael Calvert (seated second from right) at the Bush Warfare School in Maymyo, Burma in 1942. Calvert went from Australia to Burma in late 1941 as part of 204 Mission. At Maymyo, he was the chief instructor and then commandant of the commando training school, the objective of which was to raise the efficiency of the Chinese guerrillas fighting the Japanese in the technical methods of demolition and sabotage, thereby keeping Japanese divisions tied up in China and diverted from being deployed elsewhere throughout the Pacific. Orde Wingate first met Calvert there, but as the Japanese advance inexorably crept across Burma, there was no point to Wingate's staying there to foment a British-led Burmese guerrilla-style insurrection against the Japanese. As Calvert said, 'He [Wingate] had arrived too late to do anything, in any case, and there were no troops available which had not already been committed, except my Bush Warfare School personnel' (Calvert 1996: 83). (USAMHI)

two road-blocks to be established, one on either side of the railway, in order to interdict any Japanese troop patrols. Subadar Kum Singh Gurung's No. 4 Party included a Bren-gun crew and a Boys anti-tank rifle crew led by an NCO armed with a Thompson submachine gun. They were to take up a position half a mile to the north to watch the motor road from Indaw. Capt Ian MacKenzie stationed his No. 5 Party on both sides of the motor road where it crossed the *chaung* 2 miles due south of the station. This party also included a Bren-gun crew and a Boys anti-tank rifle crew, and carried mines to lay in the road should a Japanese attack materialize from Wuntho in the south. A fifth detachment, No. 3 Party, was comprised of the muleteers for the mules and an *oozie* for Flossie the elephant. This group marched through the station from the bivouac area into cover provided by a *chaung* in the jungle on the south-eastern side of the railway. The sixth detachment, Capt William 'Taffy' Griffiths' No. 6 Party, was comprised of a section of Burma Rifles and included Flt Lt Robert Thompson, who was in charge of the wireless sets for signals transmission and communication with RAF bases to co-ordinate bombing missions against Japanese troop positions at Naba, Indaw and Wuntho. Griffiths and his men were positioned to ambush any Japanese coming north on the motor road from Wuntho.

Prior to deploying his men to their assigned areas, Calvert fixed a rendezvous several miles to the south-east of the railway. After sending off his RAF wireless signals, Thompson looked at his watch. At 1245hrs, the two demolition teams moved onto the railway; at 1315hrs, the battle of Nankan was under way; and at 1400hrs, according to Thompson, 'my job was to take all the mules across the railway and road to the column rendezvous point about two miles east in the Ganzan Range, beyond which lay the Irrawaddy' (Thompson 1989: 26).

Lieutenant-General Mutaguchi's 18th Division garrisoned the area through which Wingate's columns moved. The three battalions of Colonel Koba's 55th Infantry Regiment were responsible for a large area of the

The innovative methods espoused by Wingate included the use of long-range radio communications and RAF resupply of the columns by parachuting in supplies. To ensure that both worked optimally, Wingate's columns took RAF personnel with them to co-ordinate the air drops. RAF signallers among the Chindits' ranks called for vital air resupply every few days. Here, an RAF sergeant operates an air–ground wireless set – possibly a WS TR1143 or a WS TR1196 – in a jungle bivouac. (© IWM IND 2292)

Chindits' columns trek. Elements of Major Shigemi's I/55th Infantry were stationed at Indaw. In the middle of February, this battalion was split up into small garrisons stationed at Nauangkan, Sinlamaung, Pinbon, Pinlebu, Wuntho and Indaw, with standing patrols at a number of points along the railway line. The Japanese were based in some strength at Indaw, 25 miles to the north, after Koba decided to move his regimental headquarters from Katha to Indaw with over half of I/55th Infantry under his command at the end of February after learning about the Chindit columns' dispositions.

The engagement at Nankan Station was not typical of the close-combat fighting between the Chindits and the Japanese during Operation *Longcloth*. The Chindits' major tactic was stealth, in an attempt to avoid major engagements with their more numerous and heavily armed IJA opponents. If attacked, a Chindit column in the jungle was to disperse and regroup at some pre-arranged area later. However, in this engagement, the specific task of laying demolitions by two of the columns' parties – under Calvert himself and Silcock – would require time and a defensive preparation if the Japanese appeared during this portion of the mission, at a moment when quick dispersal would prevent its completion. All the weapons utilized by both sides were well-suited to use in the open area in which the Chindit ambush would take place. Moreover, the Japanese had the potential advantage to slip into the jungle for concealment, but as was characteristic of their élan, once they deployed from their lorries, these infantrymen would opt to attack across the open ground against the numerically inferior foe. Some of the Chindit officers, who had been in Burma during the rout of 1942, identified a growing lack of aggression of the Japanese in 1943. The Japanese seemed satisfied to confine themselves to shelling positions they thought were held by Chindit forces with mortars and artillery from a distance. At Nankan Station, however, the open ground would embolden the Japanese infantrymen to resort to their aggressive attack mode and close on the enemy with the bayonet.

Two truckloads of Japanese soldiers from I/55th Infantry, accompanied by a vehicle later described by Calvert as a 'tankette', came lumbering down the motor road from Indaw head-on into Singh's No. 4 Party, positioned 1 mile north of Nankan Station to watch the road from Indaw. The first burst from the Boys killed six Japanese infantrymen as they deployed from their truck. After the trucks came under fire from Singh's ambush, additional Japanese reinforcements arrived, meaning No. 4 Party became outnumbered three-to-one. Singh was well aware that if the Japanese broke through his ambush, the two demolition parties' efforts could be nullified, and so he sent a runner back

to Griffiths' No. 6 Party, requesting reinforcements; soon they, too, entered the fray. Griffiths also sent runners to Calvert to inform him of the Japanese attack from the north and to Silcock's No. 2 Party requesting a section to reinforce the ambush. Continued fighting ensued.

The demolition groups had been working for over three-and-a-half hours when the ambush parties under Singh and Griffiths were forced to give ground – after holding their positions all afternoon – as the Japanese took control of Nankan village, whose inhabitants had fled at the first sign of gunfire. Shortly after 1530hrs, 6 miles of railway and three bridges were a complete shambles after the demolitions detonated. Lt Harold James and his platoon of Gurkhas had been escorting Calvert and his men to fix their charges and connect the fuses. A loud explosion occurred and, as James later recalled:

> The next moment Calvert was running towards me, shouting for everyone to take cover behind a bank. We scrambled over and not long afterwards there was a great roar as the bridge went up, pieces of metal flew in all directions, and a large section passed low over our heads like a fighter aircraft, screaming past to embed itself in a tree-trunk with the noise of a large drum. (Quoted in Chinnery 2010: 68)

The bridge that had been blown up by Lt Jeffrey Lockett was a three-span steel girder bridge with stone abutments stretching 120ft over a deep *chaung*. After the explosions, Calvert left Sgt Maj R.S. Blain and his men to continue demolishing the railway line at 100yd intervals. Then, accompanied by James' Gurkhas, Calvert heeded Griffiths' call and ran towards the firing to the north. His party stopped to demolish a 60ft-span bridge over a *chaung*; despite well-aimed machine-gun fire from a Japanese tankette, the Chindits laid their charges and destroyed the bridge.

At 1645hrs, a party of 50 British soldiers appeared down a track leading from the mountains. These unexpected reinforcements were Chindits armed with heavier weapons and led by Capt Petersen. Petersen explained that they 'had lost contact with the larger part of their Column 7, under the command of Major K.D. Gilkes, and for three days had marched on banana-palms, jungle roots, and a few handfuls of uncooked rice' (quoted in Rolo 1944: 77). Calvert deployed all of these men, as well as those from his No. 1 Party, and decided to attack the Japanese. He deployed his men in battle formation and by utilizing Petersen's 3in mortars destroyed a Japanese truck. Some of the Japanese infantry tried to cross the open ground to outflank the Chindits, but

A .45-calibre M1928 Thompson submachine gun. Note the top cocking handle and pistol-grip forend; here, the weapon has a 20-round box magazine, but had the capability of taking a 50-round drum magazine. Weighing 10.8lb when empty, this fine submachine gun was relatively small and easy to handle, with a barrel length of 10.5in. With a theoretical rate of fire of 800 rounds per minute, it had a devastating stopping effect in the close-quarters combat typical for the clashes on Burma's jungle tracks. The Japanese lacked submachine guns and so the availability of the Thompson – and later the 9mm Sten – gave a clear advantage to the Chindits. (Neil Grant)

Japanese troops disembarking from Nissan trucks. Unlike their Chindit adversaries, the Japanese did possess some limited motor transport – especially on the eastern side of the Irrawaddy where there were motor roads – enabling them to keep up the momentum of their pursuit of Wingate's 77th Indian Infantry Brigade during Operation *Longcloth*. Wingate violated his own principles by crossing the Irrawaddy since he now lost jungle cover to evade his pursuers – and furthermore it was intensely hot, with a paucity of fresh water. Although he had almost exceeded the distance limit for aerial transport resupply with his excursion east across the river, he did manage to get some supplies dropped to his force. During this interval, Calvert's No. 3 Column uncharacteristically attacked the enemy again, near Sitton on 23 March, killing over 100 Japanese troops who were establishing patrol stations on the roads toward the Irrawaddy re-crossing points. The next day, Wingate ordered the retreat to India. (USAMHI)

were shot down *en masse*; others fled northwards into the jungle, leaving about a third of the force from Indaw dead in the field. No. 5 Party planted booby traps along the motor road and these destroyed a light tank as well as another truck. Calvert's force did not lose a single man in this firefight.

Calvert then sent orders to all sections to make for the rallying point to the south-east near the Irrawaddy River. Subadar Singh was afterwards awarded the Indian Distinguished Service Medal for the skill and courage he displayed by leading his party's ambush while covering the demolitions on the railway. That night, Thompson received a congratulatory wireless message from Wingate in Arabic. Calvert turned to the RAF officer and said, 'Well Bob that was a hell of a good party' (quoted in Rolo 1944: 78). Calvert would receive the Distinguished Service Order several months after the successful attack on Nankan Station.

When Koba learned of the railway demolition attack at Nankan Station, he took two companies of I/55th Infantry under his own command, and hurried from Indaw to the Irrawaddy River. There he inflicted damage on Calvert's No. 3 Column as it crossed the river between Tagaung and Tigyaing on a small island. This island was about 4 miles square; it was covered in elephant grass about 8–10ft high and separated from the west bank by a narrow channel. Despite suffering casualties, Calvert with a rear-guard enabled the majority of No. 3 Column to reach the eastern bank of the Irrawaddy.

The combat between the Japanese infantrymen and the Chindits during Operation *Longcloth* was at close quarters and often consisted of small group ambushes and skirmishes. This was largely based on Wingate's maintenance of smaller groups within his columns for dedicated tasks and the Japanese limited response to them because of uncertainty of the Chindit whereabouts or destinations. At Nankan Station, Calvert's Chindits did, indeed, set up their ambushes in order to protect the demolition parties and they were fortunate that only a limited response from I/55th Infantry was on hand, since that battalion had been split up into small garrisons and standing patrols

Rear view of a disabled Type 95 *Ha-Go*, a Japanese light tank used primarily for infantry support with its low-velocity 3.7cm main turret gun and two 7.7mm machine guns making them suitable for attacking enemy pillboxes. The thin armour, although of good quality, of this and other Japanese armoured vehicles made them easy targets for even antiquated British anti-tank weapons such as Calvert's Boys anti-tank rifle and mortars, which destroyed a Japanese armoured vehicle at Nankan Station. In 1944, 2-pdr anti-tank guns flown into the 'stronghold' at White City would enable columns from 77th Indian Infantry Brigade and others to fend off Japanese light tanks as part of the IJA's all-out offensive against White City with its 24th Independent Mixed Brigade. (USAMHI)

along the railway line. Had Major Shigemi, commanding officer of I/55th Infantry, been able to concentrate larger components of his battalion on 6 March 1943 in the immediate vicinity of Nankan Station, Calvert's entire mission might have been made completely untenable or, perhaps, his entire force destroyed.

The engagement at Nankan Station was unusual for an action during Operation *Longcloth* since almost all of the combat took place in the open with clear fields of fire. Also, owing to the nature of Calvert's mission – to destroy the railway bridges and tracks, after taking approximately three hours to lay charges – Calvert's forces could not withdraw from a numerically larger foe. Up until this point, Wingate's doctrine directed that after combat was initiated with a larger Japanese force, the engaging Chindit unit was to disperse and rendezvous with the remainder of the column.

The Japanese could not concentrate their forces sufficiently because of a lack of thorough knowledge of Wingate's divided columns' whereabouts. This allowed Calvert's No. 3 Column to approach Nankan Station unmolested, and also enabled his demolition parties to conduct the bridge and railway destruction without an overwhelming Japanese force being present to attack them. The scattering of the companies of Koba's I/55th Infantry, which in aggregate comprised more than half a battalion, also ensured the Japanese had difficulty in recapturing the station and defeating the Chindit demolition teams due to their limited numbers – although at the beginning of their attack the Japanese outnumbered Singh's motor-road ambush party until Griffiths and Silcock could send additional reinforcing sections. Most importantly, the unplanned arrival of Petersen's 50 men tipped the scales to favour Calvert. Wingate recommended Petersen for a Military Cross: 'His actions in these operations proved that leadership is everything … Some officers … would have gone back to the Chindwin … Others would have blundered into the enemy. Petersen marched for the railway, outstripping everyone and arrived in Nankan railway station in the middle of a fight between the Japanese and 3 Column' (quoted in Bierman & Smith 1999: 280).

# Pagoda Hill

## 16–18 March 1944

## BACKGROUND TO BATTLE

**OPPOSITE** Chindits 'brew up' in a jungle bivouac. Not only did this break provide rest and sustenance, but for the troops being able to brew their 'char', it was a morale booster. Wingate had trained his infantrymen on forced marches in India and reinforced his tenet in the Burmese jungle for Chindit columns to break up into smaller, platoon-sized units for such rest intervals. Each platoon-sized unit would then be responsible for providing its own defensive perimeter. In this manner, columns could move into and out of designated bivouac areas quickly after having prepared food and tea, as well as unload the mules for a time interval. (© IWM IND 2289)

On 27 March 1943, Lieutenant-General Mutaguchi Renya, the 18th Division commander, was promoted to lead 15th Army in northern Burma; his successor at 18th Division was Lieutenant-General Tanaka Shinichi. Mutaguchi had scrutinized Wingate's tactics and his use of the Burmese terrain and concluded, as the Chindits had demonstrated, that troops would be mobile with pack transport only in northern and western Burma during the dry season. The Chindits had shown that it was possible for units to attack across the main north–south grain of the rivers and mountains of Burma. The Japanese general's revelation, along with intelligence of the British build-up at Imphal, convinced Mutaguchi that he must eventually attack Imphal and Kohima to pre-empt another large-scale British invasion of Burma from India in 1944. However, prior to that invasion, Mutaguchi argued that 15th Army's line of defence should be moved westwards, to at least the Chindwin River, or even possibly to the hills on the Assam–Burma border. On 11 April, Mutaguchi was relieved of the responsibility of looking after northern Burma and was given the single task of planning the Imphal/Kohima offensive, Operation *U-Go*. The best course would be to attack the British before they had time to complete their preparations for an offensive and capture their base at Imphal, thereby preventing them launching an

Japanese infantry cross a fordable river in Burma with their heavily laden mules. The Japanese were very dependent on pack animals due to inadequate motor transport, thus were forced to improvise methods to carry heavy loads of equipment on their lengthy treks. Here, the pack mules are carefully assisted out of the riverbank, which could be treacherous with deep mud and the heavy load. During the infantryman's training, every measure was instilled to protect the mule and its equipment packed onto it. Harsh discipline and even death awaited the IJA infantryman who lost a pack animal and its load due to negligence or inattention. (USAMHI)

offensive into Burma. The end of summer 1943 found the IJA planning an offensive for the dry season of early 1944.

Wingate, ever the self-promoter, wrote his report of Operation *Longcloth* while convalescing from the mission in June 1943 and sent it uncensored to one of his patrons in London, Leo Amery MP. This memorandum ultimately arrived on Churchill's desk. Although the British prime minister – hugely impressed – was talked out of appointing Wingate to lead Fourteenth Army, in August 1943 Churchill took Wingate to Quebec for the Quadrant Conference. There, Wingate presented his views about an enlarged LRP expedition for Burma in 1944, as part of a multipronged Allied offensive in southern Asia, to the Combined Chiefs of Staff and President Roosevelt. Thanks to the interest of Roosevelt and his subordinates, the US Army was to train its own LRP force

A C-47 Dakota practises towing a Waco glider. Wingate and his subordinates decided to abandon 'Piccadilly' as a landing field since teak logs were observed on aerial reconnaissance photographs literally hours before the air invasion. After a brief consultation, Wingate and Brig Calvert, commanding 77th Indian Infantry Brigade, decided to shift the brigade's landing entirely to Broadway. This necessitated Col Cochran to redirect the Dakotas and gliders, resulting in each of the C-47 aircraft being allotted two Waco gliders to tow simultaneously. The best Air Commando pilots, given good weather, could manage a double tow, but many were inexperienced and had not had enough practice. During the airlift to Broadway, reports of gliders parting from their tows or being cast off by alarmed pilots, indicated that some cargo and troop-carrying Wacos had either crashed or disappeared all along the route – from 3 miles from the edge of the Lalaghat airfield starting point, to remote forests well east of the Chindwin River. (USAMHI)

under Wingate, as well as 1st Air Commando Group from USAAF cadres, to provide the Chindits with an expanded aerial dimension to their tactical doctrine. In December 1943, after some bickering with General Headquarters at New Delhi, Wingate was to get six Chindit infantry brigades.

Wingate's expanded attack strategy was novel but realistic. Air power would revolutionize LRP, as fighter-bombers became aerial artillery and the transports and gliders provided supplies, armaments and reinforcements, as well as casualty evacuation – the latter a major missing dimension and source of low morale during Operation *Longcloth* – all enabled by state-of-the-art radio communications. Sea- or land-borne LOC for an invading force had been made unnecessary. Unlike his units in Operation *Longcloth*, Wingate envisaged Special Force, as the Chindits were to be called (or '3rd Indian Division' as it appeared in the Order of Battle), being able to stay and fight at locales of choice (i.e. at the 'strongholds'), rather than dispersing or having to fight their way back through an enclosing enemy. The Chindit leader had now brought together his tactical concept of movement in the Burmese jungle with proximate defended garrisons.

As early as 16 January 1944, Wingate provided evidence to Mountbatten that a Japanese move up to the Chindwin River was the preparatory stage for an offensive against Assam. He believed that the Japanese would be compelled to use the poor road infrastructure of western Burma. As predicted, on 14–15 March, a three-division-strong Japanese force invaded Assam from the north of Homalin and from the centre of their Chindwin front, in Operation *U-Go*. Also at that time, Wingate formulated his new tactical plan for Operation *Thursday*, which was to establish defended areas wherever his brigades were operating. The initial entry of roughly two columns into Burma would be made by aircraft and gliders. This force would occupy the landing strip and convert it into an airfield for larger transport aircraft. Then, the transport aircraft would bring in the rest of the brigade.

On the evening of 5 March 1944, Colonel Sakuma Takanobu, commanding 214th Infantry Regiment (33rd Division), saw 'huge transport aircraft, red and green navigation lights clearly visible passing overhead in what seemed like an endless procession. Must be going to bomb Rangoon' (quoted in Allen 2000: 316). A few nights later, Colonel Matsumura Hiroshi (60th Infantry Regiment, 15th Division) awoke to see transport planes towing gliders in a north-easterly direction and pondered, 'But what are they making for behind our lines?' (quoted in Allen 2000: 316). Initially, Mutaguchi offered no plans to deal with the Chindit airborne invasion. On 9 March, he received a signal estimating that the airborne force might be between 700 and 800 men strong. When Major-General Tazoe Noboru, the commander of the Japanese Air Force in Burma, asserted that Mutaguchi should hurl against them every unit he could, even if this meant postponing the Imphal operation, the bombastic 15th Army commander retorted, 'You worry too much …

You're an airman, so naturally you think it's important … What kind of strength can they muster … While they're scuttling around Katha, I'll be into Imphal and cut the line to Ledo. They'll simply wither on the vine … I'll cut at their very roots in Ledo. I've never lost a battle yet' (quoted in Allen 2000: 327). Wingate had never intended to have land-based LOC for Operation *Thursday*. His supplies and reinforcements would be furnished solely by the new aerial dimension available to him.

On 5–6 March 1944 Brig Michael Calvert's 77th Indian Infantry Brigade was inserted into the Kaukkwe Valley

A Chindit on a stretcher receives plasma at Broadway on 6 March 1944. He was one of the many casualties of the previous night's glider crashes, owing to furrows in the landing field. Out of Calvert's 542 men that landed by glider, 24 had been killed and 30 badly wounded. It is quite evident that Wingate's new paradigm for Operation *Thursday* was intended to address more pro-active medical care of the wounded in the field as well as construction of light-aircraft strips for rapid evacuation of serious cases to rear-echelon hospitals. The despondency that overtook the surviving Chindits after Operation *Longcloth*, with respect to leaving the seriously wounded or non-ambulatory troops behind, was to be avoided during this mission. The Chindit standing over the stretcher has a 9mm Sten submachine gun slung over his right shoulder. Featuring a 32-round detachable box magazine and capable of producing a cyclic rate of fire of 500 rounds per minute, it was relatively light at 6.5lb and had an overall length of 30in. Its range was limited, though, to 230ft and it had a bad tendency when used in the jungle either to jam or to fire off uncontrollably. (NARA RG-208-AA-221-50653-AC)

north-east of Katha to establish a 'stronghold' designated Broadway. In order to disrupt the Indaw–Myitkyina railway and motor-road traffic supplying 18th Division (now commanded by Lieutenant-General Tanaka Shinichi) in the Hukawng and Mogaung valleys, Calvert led his force on an arduous trek, commencing on 9 March 1944, through the Kaukkwe Valley. The force was comprised of five columns from Broadway: two columns from 3rd Battalion, 6th Gurkha Rifles, under Lt-Col Hugh Skone (No. 36) and Maj Freddie Shaw (No. 63); two columns from 1st Battalion, The South Staffordshire Regiment, under Lt-Col G.P. Richards (No. 38) and Maj Ron Degg (No. 80); and one column (No. 25), led by Calvert himself, comprised of elements of 77th Indian Infantry Brigade including Capt Ian Macpherson's Brigade HQ Defence Company, a Gurkha unit, which was Calvert's personal assault company. Calvert's mission was to establish a railway and road-block at Henu. As fit as the Chindits were, it would take Calvert's force six days to traverse the jungles and coax their supply-laden mules over the Gangaw Range to the east of Henu.

Mutaguchi had no contingency plans for an Allied airborne invasion and he was going to use only whatever Japanese units were on hand in the area of the landings to oppose the Chindits. In the Henu area, Mutaguchi had: two companies of Japanese troops from a railway engineer battalion and assorted administrative troops at Henu village; three sections of a platoon (under 2nd Lieutenant Kiyomizu) from Major Takemura's II/51st Infantry (15th Division); and two infantry companies formed from elements of III/114th Infantry (18th Division) and led by Lieutenant-Colonel Nagahashi Jiroku of Mutaguchi's HQ staff, stationed in the area Mandalay–Maymyo; 500 rear-echelon troops garrisoned at Mawlu village and Mawlu Station; and 300 Japanese infantry from assorted units at Nansiaung, just north of Henu.

**MAP KEY**

**1  Afternoon, 16 March:** Having left Broadway on 9 March for their seven-day trek across the Kaukkwe Valley and Gangaw Range, Richards' No. 38 Column and Degg's No. 80 Column of 1st South Staffordshire reach the railway at Henu first, and attempt to dig in on a nearby hill.

**2  Afternoon, 16 March:** Lt-Col Skone's No. 36 Column arrives at Henu.

**3  Evening, 16 March:** Lt Norman Durant posts his Vickers machine-gun platoon and a rifle company platoon from No. 80 Column at the foot of a hill adjacent to Pagoda Hill, where the Japanese are surreptitiously digging entrenchments.

**4  Dawn, 17 March:** Durant investigates Pagoda Hill and discovers Japanese troops digging in; he initiates a firefight.

**5  Dawn, 17 March:** 2nd Lieutenant Kiyomizu's three sections of his platoon of II/51st Infantry (15th Division) advance onto a hill adjacent to Pagoda Hill. At 1100hrs, heavy rifle fire and light-machine-gun fire is directed at Durant's men from Pagoda Hill and another nearby hill where Kiyomizu's platoon has taken up position.

**6  1600hrs, 17 March:** Having led his Brigade HQ into the valley to meet Shaw's No. 63 Column, Calvert and six platoons of Gurkhas from the Brigade HQ Defence Company – with Gurkhas of Shaw's No. 63 Column providing covering fire –

begin to charge from OP Hill to the east onto and up Pagoda Hill, with many of the South Staffords attacking as well.

**7  1630hrs, 17 March:** The Japanese defenders get up from their positions and counter-attack. Kiyomizu's platoon-sized force is driven off by 3/6th Gurkha Rifles. At the top of the hill, a ferocious hand-to-hand combat commences in which Durant is wounded in the knee and Lt George Cairns, the South Staffords mortar officer, suffers grievous wounds but continues fighting; Kiyomizu is killed.

**8  Dusk, 17 March:** With the Japanese still holding the top of Pagoda Hill, Calvert leads another charge and the Japanese retreat into the village of Henu, followed by the Gurkhas and South Staffords, who use flamethrowers to neutralize Japanese hiding in village dugouts. The remaining Japanese flee across the rice paddy fields to the west, and the Chindits start digging in ready to face a counter-attack.

**9  17/18 March:** Before the block has been firmly established, a small enemy force, the composite Nagahashi Unit, attacks from the south. Calvert's men pour mortar and machine-gun fire into the hapless Japanese, most of whom are killed in the first few minutes; Nagahashi himself succumbs to his wounds. The Japanese attack is driven off after savage hand-to-hand fighting and several bayonet charges. Tools, barbed wire and ammunition are air-dropped into the British position; the battle of Pagoda Hill is over.

## Battlefield environment

The Kaukkwe Valley is composed of a dank, dark jungle of primeval growth, which would slow up any force marching through it. The Gangaw Range of mountains, to the east of Henu, has elevations between 2,900ft and 4,500ft from the vicinity of Mawlu in the south to Mawhun, north of Henu. The countryside around Henu opens up into dry rice paddies during this time of the year and marsh near towns and villages. Everywhere else is covered by jungle. Henu is a village about a mile north-west of Mawlu and its railway station. At the village, there is a cluster of about seven foothills (including Pagoda Hill, Bare Hill, OP Hill) between 30ft and 50ft in height, with numerous valleys in between. OP Hill offered a good view of the surrounding countryside, with Pagoda Hill lying to the west between

the motor road and railway. To the north of OP Hill was Bare Hill, where all the trees had been cut down and lay as logs all over it. Calvert's block at Henu was ideally situated around this series of wooded hills with water at the north and south extremities. The brigadier included the village of Henu within the defended perimeter; all the mules and the Brigade HQ were brought into it.

A wingtip of an Allied transport (top) can be seen as white parachutes drift down towards a jungle-clad ridge in the Gangaw Range; supplies are being air-dropped to columns of 77th Indian Infantry Brigade at Henu after the surrounding lower-elevation hills, including Pagoda Hill, had been secured as a Chindit 'stronghold'. The trees surrounding Henu became festooned with the white parachutes that became ensnared in the branches, prompting the name 'White City'. (© IWM IND 7075)

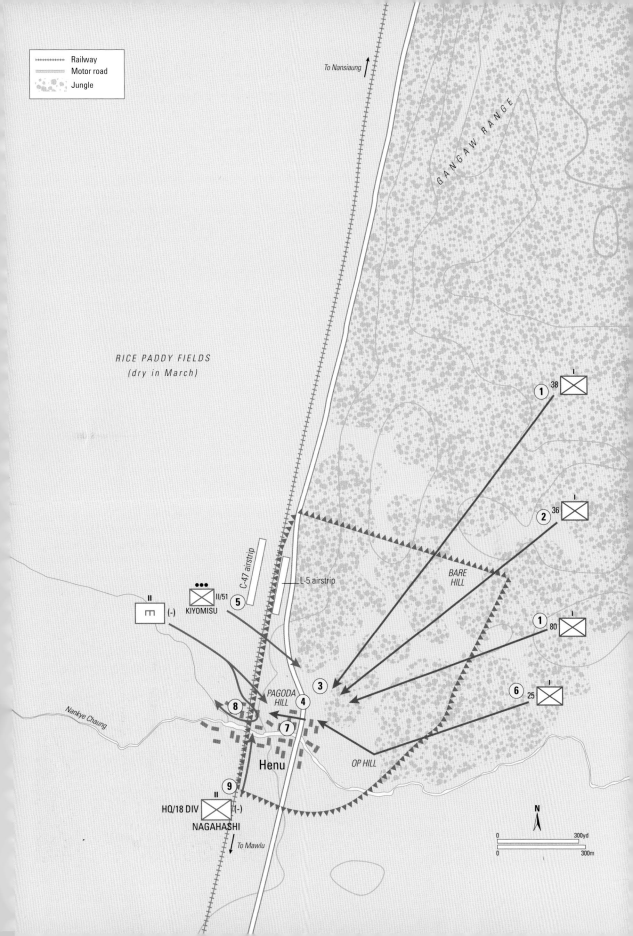

Railway
Motor road
Jungle

To Nansiaung

GANGAW RANGE

RICE PADDY FIELDS
(dry in March)

1 38

2 36

BARE
HILL

1 80

C-47 airstrip

L-5 airstrip

KIYOMISU II/51 5

II (-)

3

6 25

PAGODA
HILL

4

8

7

Nankye Chaung

OP HILL

Henu

9

HQ/18 DIV II (-)
NAGAHASHI

To Mawlu

N

0        300yd
0        300m

# INTO COMBAT

At 2100hrs on 15 March, Lt Hugh Patterson and his commando platoon of 1st Lancashire Fusiliers laid their demolition charges on the Mawhun railway bridge. The leading troops of the five Chindit columns began arriving in the vicinity of Henu late in the morning of 16 March. During the afternoon, the remainder of Richards' No. 38 Column and Degg's No. 80 Column reached the railway and started to entrench there with only a portion of the picks, shovels, ammunition and barbed wire that had been parachuted in prior to their arrival. The Gurkhas of Skone's No. 36 Column were next to take up position at the railway, while Shaw's No. 63 Column put in a diversionary holding attack on the Japanese troops at Nansiaung, just to the north of Henu village, on the railway. Two platoons of Shaw's Gurkhas would return to Calvert's assistance as a reserve on Pagoda Hill the next day.

Calvert chose Henu as a site for a railway and motor-road block after an aerial reconnaissance. He reasoned that the area he had chosen was ideal for a blocking position on the road and rail track at Mawlu since it dominated both the railway heading north from Mawlu and the surrounding area. The road and railway ran next to each other at Henu and a block could be placed astride them simultaneously. Thus, the road and rail traffic leading up to Mogaung and Myitkyina could be disrupted. In addition, there was water nearby that could be included in a defensive perimeter, and flat land to construct a Stinson L-5 Sentinel airstrip for evacuation of the wounded as well as a C-47 Dakota transport airstrip to bring in supplies, reinforcements, animals and ordnance for defence of the block. As the days passed, the supply planes would festoon the high trees around the block at Henu with white parachutes, hence the name 'White City'.

As evening approached, Lt Durant, commanding a machine-gun platoon in Degg's No. 80 Column, had his guns posted on one of the seven little hills in the Henu area, with two platoons of the column's rifle company at the base of the hill. Nearby was a higher foothill called Pagoda Hill, because of the temple structure at the top of it. The Chindits had not occupied this hill, and were unaware at the time that the Japanese had silently taken up positions there. Both sides were hastily preparing basic field fortifications in ignorance of the other side's close proximity.

Chindits with shovels smooth furrows on Broadway's landing field on 6 March 1944. A small bulldozer with an attached scraper, which survived the original glider crashes caused by these furrows in the field, works hastily in the background to construct a safer airstrip. This labour facilitated further landings by Waco gliders, which reinforced the Chindit troop strength, and eventually C-47 Dakotas at Broadway, enabling a rapid build-up and defence of the 'stronghold' against an anticipated IJA infantry and air attack. Some other Waco gliders became unattached from their C-47 Dakotas on the way to Broadway and crash-landed in either western Burma or Assam. This unfortunate event serendipitously created an unplanned diversion and caused Japanese attention to shift away from the landing zones to the remote glider crash sites. (NARA C-993134)

At dawn on 17 March, Durant was told by Sgt John C. Jenkins, serving in the column's rifle company, that a lot of noise in a foreign language was coming from Pagoda Hill. He thought it was some local Burmese villagers. Durant walked to the foot of Pagoda Hill to gauge which 'locals were yammering' (quoted in Bidwell 1979: 119). The 'locals' were in fact a few Japanese soldiers, who were unaware of the Chindit presence from the night before. Durant seized a Bren gun and started a firefight with the Japanese there, who responded with heavy-machine-gun and medium mortar fire.

Coincident with this, 2nd Lieutenant Kiyomizu's three lightly armed sections dropped off their packs and came in for the attack through the morning mist onto Hill D, adjacent to Pagoda Hill, to infiltrate between Degg's and Skone's columns. Takemura ordered Kiyomizu to take his platoon to Mawlu, estimating the airborne contingent there to number about 1,000. Kiyomizu had not anticipated how strong the Chindit positions would be in contrast to his underserved platoon as he made for Pagoda Hill via Hill D. Durant's post-war account stated that:

Leading their mule train, British infantrymen cross the Nankye Chaung on their way from Broadway to Mawlu during Operation *Thursday*. The reliance on pack animals for hauling heavy equipment was imperative for the Chindit columns. In these columns, 'first line' mules would carry the heavier weapons and ammunition used by the rifle sections while 'second line' pack animals would transport the heavy wireless sets, additional ammunition, and other items necessary for the conduct of the campaign. Wingate had insisted that animal transport officers and muleteers keep the animals healthy, but many succumbed to Japanese fire. (NARA RG-208-AA-221-SE262 RN)

> At about 1100 hrs, heavy rifle fire and L.M.G. fire opened up on us from hill C – Pagoda Hill – and at the same time we came under grenade and mortar fire from hill D where a Jap Pl. had taken up position. For the next 4 hours we had a very unpleasant time indeed. We couldn't see the Japs and there were very few parts of the hill that weren't under fire. Casualties were mounting up. I had to move the Vickers every half hour or so as the Jap was doing his best to knock them out. He put a burst across one gun which hit the man firing it in the thigh, another in the foot and ripped the box of ammunition which was being made into shreds. However, we silenced one of their L.M.G.'s and from occasional screams knew that we were also inflicting casualties. By now a third of us were casualties, including the rifle Coy. 2nd-in-C who was hit in both feet, and one of the Pl. commanders who got a bullet through the buttocks, and we were extremely glad to get a message over the wireless to say that the Brigadier was on his way with 2 companies of Gurkhas and would counter attack any feature held by the Japs. The next hour was absolute hell. The Japs stepped up their mortaring and grenading and it became quite obvious that at any moment they might rush the road and attack from Pagoda Hill. (Quoted in Bidwell 1979: 119–20)

At about 1600hrs, Calvert and his six platoons of Gurkhas, which comprised his own crack Gurkha Brigade HQ Defence Company, rushed toward the gunfire. It was evident that the men of 1st South Staffordshire were not dug in properly and were in full view of the enemy. Calvert personally got to a ridge to investigate the combat activity and observed the Japanese milling about a pagoda on top of a little knoll. On another small hill, lower down and near the road, were the South Staffords with mortar bombs exploding around them. The Chindits were trying to retaliate with their Vickers machine guns and their own mortars, but they were without much cover, with the Japanese controlling the high ground in the immediate vicinity. Calvert immediately assessed the desperate nature of the situation, since it appeared to him that the Japanese had seized the initiative and were about to thwart his plan to establish the road and rail block at Henu village. The brigadier began to charge from

## Nagahashi Jiroku

One of Mutaguchi's staff officers in March 1944, Lieutenant-Colonel Nagahashi had served in 18th Division as a junior officer during the Malay campaign, culminating in the capture of Singapore in February 1942. The following month, Nagahashi was sent to Burma as 18th Division was attached to the Burma Army. In May 1942, after the conquest of Burma was completed, he was given the command of 22nd Cavalry Battalion within 18th Division. In late 1943, Nagahashi headed an 80-man 'Special Intelligence Party' in the Hukawng Valley near Taro, where 18th Division's 56th Infantry Regiment was combatting Stilwell's Chinese troops. With the commencement of Operation *Thursday* in March 1944, Nagahashi was sent to Indaw to assemble two infantry companies from III/114th Infantry. These companies were to be designated as the Nagahashi Unit, a provisional composite battalion of troops, which was en route from Kyaukme to Myitkyina. Their orders were simply to attack the enemy where they found them. Nagahashi found Calvert and put in a night attack on his force at White City on 17 March. Calvert lit up the night sky with star shells and poured mortar bombs and machine-gun fire into the men of the Nagahashi Unit, most of whom were killed in the first few minutes of the attack. Nagahashi himself died of his wounds while leading the assault.

OP Hill to the east, across a paddy and up Pagoda Hill with many of the South Staffords attacking as well, while Shaw's returning Gurkha platoons gave him covering fire. Calvert stated many years after the war:

> Standing up, I shouted out 'Charge' in the approved Victorian manner, and ran down the hill with Bobbie [Sqn Ldr Robert Thompson] and two orderlies. Half of the South Staffords joined in. Then looking back I found a lot had not. So I told them to bloody well 'Charge! What the hell do you think you're doing?' So they all charged, the machine-gunners, mortar teams, the officers – all who were on the hill. As we climbed Pagoda Hill, the Japs, entering into the spirit of the thing, got up and charged us. (Quoted in Chinnery 1997: 129)

2nd Lieutenant Kiyomizu's platoon-sized Japanese force was driven off by men of 3/6th Gurkha Rifles. During the hand-to-hand combat, Kiyomizu was struck in the right arm and genitals while using his sword, and died. Calvert observed that at the top of Pagoda Hill, 'about fifty yards square, an extraordinary melee took place, everyone shooting, bayoneting, kicking at everyone else, rather like an officers' guest night' (quoted in Chinnery 1997: 129). Durant caught sight

## John B. Jefferies

John Jefferies was a Royal Navy officer for nine years before resigning his commission. When war broke out, he joined The Royal Ulster Rifles and was commissioned a 2nd lieutenant after serving in the ranks for six months. He then joined the fledgling Commandos in August 1940 and saw action during several missions. After volunteering for special duty in the Far East, he was attached to Wingate's Chindits as a demolitions expert in command of No. 142 Commando Group. In February 1943, at a more southern crossing of the Chindwin River, Jefferies – now a major – while barking out orders dressed in a brigadier's uniform and insignia, successfully acted out his principal task of deceiving the Japanese that his party was Wingate's main (Northern Group) body of the expedition.

In March 1944, Jefferies fought at Pagoda Hill. After capturing the hill, Calvert's columns dug in, anticipating a Japanese counter-attack on his new perimeter. As the new Japanese assault began, Jefferies led the efforts to drive the infiltrating Japanese from the Chindit perimeter. Lt Durant of the South Staffords listened to Jefferies' last words on his portable radio: 'I'm going in now, so will close down' (quoted in Bidwell 1979: 123). Jefferies was among seven Chindit officers who died leading from the front atop Pagoda Hill.

of Calvert at the moment of the charge and noted, 'He came striding up to our hill, rifle and bayonet in hand, took a quick look around and then said to Major [John] Jefferies, "How many men can you spare to attack Pagoda Hill?" "About twenty." "Right, we'll go straight up"' (quoted in Chinnery 1997: 129). As the fighting intensified, Durant later wrote,

> [Lt] George Cairns, the mortar officer and I, hearing this, picked up some grenades, got out our revolvers and prepared to go too. We had been shot at all day, and everyone felt like getting into the Japs and exacting a bit of retribution, besides which I was very keen to see just how many casualties my machine guns had inflicted on the enemy … To this day I'm not quite certain what I expected to see – the place deserted, or the Japs on the run, I suppose – but what I actually saw was a Jap section climbing out of their trenches under the nearest house and coming straight for me, the leading two with bayonets fixed and rather unfriendly expressions, being about 20 yds. on my right. I fired my revolver and nothing happened – I was later to find that the hammer had worked loose … I realized that my sergeant [Jenkins] was a good 30 yds. behind me, out of sight round the corner, and the men with him were probably a bit behind that; time was too short for them to be of any help. I had a 4 second grenade in my hand but it was obviously useless against the two leading Japs because in considerably less than 4 second they were going to be embarrassingly close. I also knew that if I stopped or turned round I was asking to be shot. This didn't leave me very much choice of action, so I took the pin out of the grenade and, still running forward, threw it over the heads of the first two amongst the Japs who were scrambling out from under the house … and took a flying leap over the side of the hill. (Quoted in Bidwell 1979: 120–21)

A group of Japanese infantrymen ready themselves for an attack with fixed bayonets. Many are wearing their steel helmets over their field caps. The lead soldier has attached a Rising Sun battle flag with inscriptions from his family or townspeople as a good omen. The IJA infantryman in the foreground has a light machine gun, which could also have a bayonet attached to it for the close combat that was rigorously instilled into all of Imperial Japan's combat troops. (USAMHI)

Durant, Jenkins and two Chindit riflemen had been combatting Japanese soldiers who had got up from their entrenched positions beneath some Burmese houses and counter-attacked the Chindits. Durant was wounded in the knee while his sergeant with two or three other riflemen shot the leading two Japanese soldiers. The hand grenade that Durant had tossed caused some additional Japanese casualties as the remaining members of the section of enemy soldiers from the trench moved back to the opposite side of Pagoda Hill. As Durant made his way back up the hill along a path, he saw a hand-to-hand struggle occurring:

> George Cairns, the mortar officer and a Jap officer were struggling and choking on the ground, and as I picked up a Jap rifle and climbed up towards them I saw George break free and, picking up a rifle, bayonet the Jap again and again like a madman. It was only then when I got near that I saw he himself had already been bayoneted twice through the side and that his left arm was hanging on by a few strips of muscle. (Quoted in Chinnery 1997: 130)

# The fight at Pagoda Hill

In the late, clear afternoon of 17 March 1944, Lt Durant has led a small party up the side of Pagoda Hill to clear some raised huts with Japanese entrenched underneath them. Durant and his men are exhausted after five hours of receiving gunfire. Carrying only a six-shot Webley revolver in his right hand and a Mills grenade in his left, Durant is several yards ahead of his platoon sergeant, who has a Sten submachine gun. Near the hill's summit and in the open, Durant turns to his right and sees a Japanese section of six soldiers in full kit climbing from their trench under a nearby hut. Durant aims his revolver while running, but cannot fire the pistol due to a loose hammer. Clearly seeing that his platoon sergeant remains several yards behind in between two other huts, which obscured him from the two leading Japanese soldiers, Durant will hurl his grenade and swerve to his left to leap over the side of the hill several feet away.

Despite his wounds, Cairns continued to swing the Japanese officer's sword and inflict further casualties on the Japanese infantrymen. Cairns would shortly expire from his wounds, but – as Calvert noted at his side, when death was near – said: 'Have we won, Sir? Was it all right? Did we do our stuff? Don't worry about me' (quoted in Chinnery 1997: 130). Cairns received a posthumous Victoria Cross after the war for his bravery and ceaseless individual combat despite grievous wounds.

At dusk, after the vicious hand-to-hand combat, the Japanese were still holding the top of Pagoda Hill. Calvert personally led another charge and the enemy began retreating into Henu village, followed by the Chindits, who used flamethrowers to neutralize Japanese hiding in village dugouts. The remaining Japanese fled across the rice paddy fields to the west. The Chindits started digging in furiously and laid barbed wire to ready themselves to face a counter-attack from the Japanese. In Calvert's own words, 'The fighting had been not unlike that depicted in scenes from ancient battles in the closeness of the hand-to-hand grappling before the Japs finally broke' (quoted in Calvert 1996: 51).

During the night of 17/18 March, before the White City 'stronghold' had been firmly established, a new enemy force threatened Calvert's position. The composite Nagahashi Unit was attacking. On 10 March Mutaguchi dispatched towards Indaw Lieutenant-Colonel Nagahashi's composite unit, two companies strong and formed from units of the 18th Division stationed in the Mandalay–Maymyo area; Nagahashi's orders were simply to attack the enemy where he found them. Nagahashi's force found Calvert at Henu, site of the future 'White City', and put in a night attack on 17/18 March. These Japanese infantrymen were from III/114th Infantry; unlike the Japanese combatants from earlier in the day, who gave an excellent account of themselves, Nagahashi's troops were not engineer or rear-echelon personnel. Rather, they were members of Lieutenant-General Tanaka's vaunted 18th Division. Calvert lit up the night sky with star shells and poured mortars and machine-gun fire into the hapless Japanese, most of whom were killed in the first few minutes. Nagahashi himself died from his wounds. The attack was driven off after savage hand-to-hand fighting and several bayonet charges, and then the whole area was secured for the Chindits. Calvert was told that Nagahashi's men had nothing more lethal than the misnamed 'knee mortars', which were grenade launchers in effect.

Although Calvert was pleased that his columns had won their first victory over the Japanese, it had been achieved at the cost of three South Staffordshire officers killed and four wounded (out of 14 officers who participated in the charge), plus 20 other ranks killed and 60 wounded. Calvert's men counted 42 dead Japanese, including four officers. More Japanese were shot and killed or wounded by Chindit machine guns as they struggled across the open paddy. By nightfall on 18 March, tools, barbed wire and ammunition were air-dropped into the block to secure the perimeter. The Chindits anticipated more attacks in the ensuing days since additional elements from III/114th Infantry were identified by Chindit patrol activity in the vicinity of White City. These Japanese infantry units, which had been stationed in the Sagaing area near Mandalay, had also been ordered to restore order to the situation at Henu and in the hills north-east of Mawlu. Under their commander, Colonel Yamashita, these additional Japanese infantrymen, in more than company strength, came up south of Henu on 17 March and took over what was left of Nagahashi's companies; they would attack Calvert on 21 March, only to be repulsed with heavy casualties.

So what was the outcome of the action at Pagoda Hill? 2nd Lieutenant Yoshino Shuichiro, a trained pharmacist of 11th Epidemic Prevention and Water Supply Unit (18th Division), noted about the Chindit expedition in northern Burma:

Lt George Cairns of The Somerset Light Infantry (Prince Albert's), attached to 1st Battalion, South Staffordshire Regiment, was awarded a posthumous Victoria Cross for gallantry at Pagoda Hill on 17 March 1944. Cairns' pre-war experience did not hint at the valour he would exhibit on Pagoda Hill. He was not a professional soldier and, in fact, worked in a bank, until he enlisted and received a commission in 1941. Under the strains of close combat, with one's fellow soldiers' lives in jeopardy, unusual acts of bravery were often exhibited. (© IWM HU 2052)

> In November 1943 our unit went to the Hukawng Valley, in the north of Burma, with 18 Division who were fighting the Chinese–American forces under General Stilwell … I worked hard to detect disease and supply clean water to the fighting soldiers. When the supplies were cut off by the long-range penetration groups commanded by General Orde Wingate, we Japanese had to retreat gradually. And food became scarce, so that we had to live on local yams and bamboo sprouts from the fields. This made me weak and I had to spend two months at a field hospital. (Quoted in Nunneley & Tamayama 2000: 242–43)

It was becoming evident that the interdiction of the 18th Division's LOC by the Chindit 'strongholds' and block at Henu not only impeded much-needed infantry reinforcements to Lieutenant-General Tanaka in the Hukawng and Mogaung valleys, but also severely impacted on the fighting ability and élan of the once-feared 'jungle superman', the Japanese infantryman. Not only was weakness due to disease and malnutrition evident, but insufficient amounts of ammunition was lessening the offensive spirit of the Japanese troops, often compelling them to await Allied attacks in their fortified bunkers. Not all of the soldiers were now willing to be adherent to the *bushidō* code and fight to the death, as was observed when Japanese infantrymen were willing to surrender.

What if Mutaguchi had heeded the advice about the importance of the Chindit airborne invasion from his own Japanese airmen? Rather than committing units piecemeal to disrupting a Chindit railway and motor-road block at Henu, he could have mounted a reinforced attack on the position early and dealt Calvert's columns a lethal blow. Instead, very few troops, if any, were diverted from his Operation *U-Go* to reinforce Tanaka's 18th Division. Mutaguchi's subordinates either disposed their troops ineffectively, such as attacking in small groups, or scattered geographically to cover large areas of

A captured Japanese soldier of the 18th Division holds onto his mess cup. He does not appear extremely malnourished, nor is his uniform in tatters. He was taken prisoner by Stilwell's Chinese troops near Lakyan Ga in the Hukawng Valley in late February 1944, a few weeks before Calvert captured Henu at Pagoda Hill. With the ensuing development of the 'stronghold' at White City, interruption of railway and motor-road supplies and reinforcements to Tanaka's 55th and 56th Infantry regiments in the Hukawng Valley started to take its toll on the Japanese infantryman's nourishment, ammunition and morale in that sector. (NARA 111-SC-263240)

northern Burma. Why did Nagahashi put in a hasty attack on the night of 17/18 March after Calvert had evicted the rear-echelon troops from Pagoda Hill? Other elements of III/114th Infantry, under Colonel Yamashita, appeared on the battlefield on 17 March. One has to wonder about the possible outcome at Henu if both III/114th Infantry contingents had been able to attack Calvert's perimeter together. As to Tanaka's scattering of 18th Division units, it is summed up best by Private Fujino Hideo:

> After transfer to Myitkyina [in 1943], the three battalions of the [114th Infantry] regiment were dispersed to three quarters. The 1st Battalion was sent to the border between Burma and China [to keep in contact with the *Tatsu* or 'Dragon' 56th Division], the 3rd to the Hukawng Valley, and only the 1000 numerical strength of our 2nd Battalion to remain at the town [Myitkyina]. (Fujino 1964: i)

From the standpoint of the Japanese infantryman, in March–May 1944 the activities of Wingate's Special Force further exacerbated the hardships and deprivations suffered by the troops of 18th Division. Private Saukichi Hirai, a rifleman in III/114th Infantry, had previously learned to fear the 'Gurkha soldier' during Operation *Longcloth*: 'Suddenly, mortar grenades exploded all around and we all run into the jungle, while palm leaves and splinters fly everywhere … These skirmishes are common and generally the enemy reappears at our rearguard with swift incursions, delivering plenty of casualties … Only momentarily do we forget the Chindit incursions and the frightening Gurkhas' (quoted in Sáiz 2011: 23). A year later, during Operation *Thursday*, Saukichi's battlefield nightmares were augmented: 'The worst was still to come. We have no supplies, our ships don't arrive, our air force has disappeared, and we have become easy prey on roads, in hamlets, and on railways. The enemy's air-planes constantly harass us and we are forced to take cover in the jungle, where humidity and insects destroy our health and equipment' (quoted in Sáiz 2011: 24).

As for the Chindits, their evolution as a LRP force had involved a paradigm shift in their tactical doctrine, largely based on the positioning of heavily defended 'strongholds' with airstrips, and the aerial dimension provided by 1st Air Commando Group to provide reinforcements and supplies and evacuate the wounded. The Chindits would no longer disperse when confronting the Japanese in the jungle. Instead, they would contest them in the jungles or withstand their headlong, often suicidal assaults on their 'strongholds'. However, with time this change in doctrine would produce 'mission creep', especially after Wingate's death on 24 March 1944. From then on, the Chindits would be employed more and more like conventional infantry, by their theatre commander Lt Gen Joseph W. Stilwell, in the seizure of Japanese positions rather than in their dedicated mode as LRP light infantry.

# Mogaung

## 2–12 June 1944

## BACKGROUND TO BATTLE

Wingate died in a fiery plane crash on 24 March 1944 and Maj-Gen Lentaigne assumed command of the Chindits a few days later. Marking a bold and offensive change in both Chindit strategy and tactics, Lentaigne's plan called for the establishment of a new block in early May, Blackpool, garrisoned by Maj Jack Masters' 111th Indian Infantry Brigade. Replacing White City,

A Japanese infantryman shooting with his Arisaka Type 38 rifle from behind a breastwork composed of thick vegetation and a dirt mound. This weapon, the standard infantry rifle, had a bolt-action system and was fed by clips with a capacity of five 6.5mm rounds; it weighed 9.1lb, which was relatively light given its greater length. An Arisaka Type 99 rifle using a 7.7mm cartridge was developed for greater effectiveness with the heavier round, and was also 6.3in shorter than the Type 38. (USAMHI)

A World War I veteran, Lt-Col W.D.A. 'Joe' Lentaigne commanded 1st Battalion, 4th Gurkha Rifles during the Burma retreat, leading many bayonet charges in order to save his men and thwart the advancing Japanese. For this, he earned a Distinguished Service Order and command of 63rd Indian Infantry Brigade. After *Longcloth*, Wavell selected him to form 111th Indian Infantry Brigade as a second Chindit-styled LRP unit. Wingate was not involved and, thus, irked because he viewed Lentaigne as an orthodox Gurkha officer who hardly supported the Chindit originator's methods. After Wingate's death Brig Derek Tulloch – Special Force's Brigadier General Staff and one of Wingate's closest friends – recommended Lentaigne to succeed Wingate and Lt-Gen Slim, another Gurkha officer, agreed at once. Many Chindits adamantly believed that Lentaigne was a fateful choice, since under his leadership the LRP concept was abandoned and Wingate's guidelines on 'strongholds' radically altered. Also, Lentaigne – under Stilwell's direction – was blamed for Calvert's Chindits being 'slaughtered like sheep' at Mogaung. The majority of Chindit casualties would occur after Lentaigne changed the scope of the Chindit LRP mission to a conventional infantry one. However, other Chindits – like Col Claude Fairweather, who stayed on at Special Force HQ as chief signals officer after Wingate's death – supported Lentaigne. Fairweather said, 'I knew Joe Lentaigne well. There is no truth that Joe was responsible for keeping his exhausted 111 Bde in the jungle after "Blackpool". It was "Vinegar" Joe Stilwell who kept them there. With the help of Lord Mountbatten, Joe Lentaigne got them out. Joe Lentaigne was a very likable man, a very gallant commander of his splendid Gurkha brigade' (quoted in Chinnery 1997: 233). (© IWM IND 3426)

Blackpool was intended to deny the Japanese the use of 'Railway Valley' – the Allied name for the area, 160 miles long, through which the railway line ran from Mawlu to where it opened up into the Mogaung Valley – and prevent Japanese reinforcements from reaching Mogaung and Myitkyina until 1 June. Lentaigne hoped that by that time, Stilwell's Chinese troops would have broken through 18th Division's front and would meet the northerly advancing Chindits on the Mogaung–Myitkyina line, thereby completing Special Force's mission. It was reasoned that with the arrival of the monsoon rains in mid-May, the Chindit 'strongholds' at White City and 'Aberdeen' – the latter established in March by Brig Fergusson and situated on the headwaters of the Meza River, 25 miles north-west of Indaw – would become untenable since they lacked all-weather airfields, which would be vital during the wet season for reinforcement, resupply and evacuation of sick and wounded.

Calvert consolidated the remaining Chindits of 77th Indian Infantry Brigade into three battalions – comprising the men of 1st Battalion, The South Staffordshire Regiment, 1st Battalion, The Lancashire Fusiliers and 3rd Battalion, 6th Gurkha Rifles – on their departure from Broadway and White City. During May 1944, they were to remain stationed opposite Blackpool in the Gangaw Range, east of the railway. Calvert was disappointed with this redeployment since he felt that White City could have held out indefinitely and it was poor form to surrender land bought with such a high price in Chindits' blood. By mid-May, Calvert had lost 38 officers and 592 other ranks killed, wounded or evacuated. Also, Blackpool was not as well defended as White City was, so by 25 May this newer block had to be evacuated under strong Japanese attack. Blackpool had achieved a desired effect of strangling the main Japanese supply route for over two weeks, but its abandonment enabled the Japanese to move 4,500–5,000 infantry with artillery towards both Mogaung and Myitkyina.

Meanwhile, after marching over the Kumon Range, on 17 May Stilwell's Sino-American force captured the Myitkyina airfield, west of the town, in a *coup de main*. From a strategic standpoint, Stilwell no longer wanted the Chindits to attract the enemy's attention away from his men, but rather – while still blocking the railway – to focus the Chindit main effort against the town of Mogaung, which threatened Stilwell's LOC to the west of the Myitkyina airfield. With the continued Chinese advance down the Kamaing road, 18th Division was in grave danger, especially if Mogaung was to be captured by the Allies. On 29 May, Calvert signalled his desire to Lentaigne to remain in his position in the Gangaw Range and resume guerrilla or LRP methods to harass the Japanese. Calvert summed up his reluctance to become conventional infantry for Stilwell: 'Therefore suggest we do *not* repeat *not* make flat-out attack against Mogaung in which we risk everything. Can this be given earnest consideration? Only way we can be defeated is by hammering our heads against a brick wall' (quoted in Bidwell 1979: 263). Lentaigne responded, 'You will take Mogaung with 77th Brigade, less 81 and 82 Columns and levies. Plan at your discretion. Ensure adequate ammunition. Give timings' (quoted in Bidwell 1979: 263). In order to secure Mogaung, Calvert wanted to have a 'secure base' that could be easily defended from Japanese counter-attack. In a repeat of his block at Henu, he wanted to build a light aircraft strip, a drop zone for supplies, a hospital and ammunition dumps. Since he would not have conventional artillery, he would have to rely upon 3in mortars. His brigade was to use approximately 60,000 mortar bombs in the capture of Mogaung. Even so, everything would depend on air support, since this would constitute Calvert's response to the firepower of 18th Division's artillery in Mogaung. In order to direct air strikes properly, Calvert would need to secure high ground – offering both improved visibility and longer radio-transmission ranges – from which his RAF liaison officers could control the sorties and make adjustments.

At Mogaung, the original Chindit organization – two columns, each acting independently, formed out of one battalion in order to conduct guerrilla warfare efficiently – would now be reversed, and two columns were merged into one battalion. According to Jeffrey:

> In the end the battalion consisted of two rifle companies, a support group of mortars and machine guns, a commando section, reconnaissance units, headquarters, and the enormous administrative group. We had two main weaknesses. In the first place, we had far too few riflemen, on whom the main burden of battle must fall: the capture of a fortified town such as Mogaung involved constant patrolling, raids and probing attacks as well as the assault itself. Equally serious was our lack of weapons of heavier calibre than a three-inch mortar which was admirable enough for breaking enemy groups in the open and neutralizing areas of jungle, but ineffective against sandbagged bunkers or pill boxes. In the Block [Broadway and White City], guns had been flown in to strengthen our defences, but we could not carry them into the hills. (Jeffrey 1950: 127)

Even after Stilwell's capture of Myitkyina airfield on 17 May, it was possible for the Japanese to move in and out of Myitkyina town in spite of the American and Chinese encirclement:

> [A] Staff Officer (Intelligence) of 33 Army, Major Mihashi, had penetrated the defences, talked with Mizukami and [Colonel] Maruyama [Fusayasu, at Myitkyina], then returned to report. It was perfectly feasible for Takeda's 53 Division, once 111 Brigade had abandoned 'Blackpool', to move through Mogaung and reinforce Myitkyina. In fact, Honda ordered him to do just that, then cancelled the order when [Lieutenant-General] Takeda [Kaoru] was within a few miles of his goal. Honda by that time judged that 18 Division's need was the greater, and since the rescue of 18 Division bulked larger in his mind than that of Myitkyina, he sent Takeda towards Kamaing; then told him to fend off the Chindit descent on Mogaung. (Allen 2000: 369)

Lt Gen Joseph W. Stilwell (left) and FM Sir Archibald P. Wavell meet at General Headquarters in New Delhi, India for a strategy conference in October 1942. The initial command structure in the China–Burma–India (CBI) theatre produced a sharp contrast and clash of wills between these two Allied leaders, which led to a political–diplomatic rift. Whereas Stilwell was an outspoken – and somewhat profane – acerbic Anglophobe, Wavell's personality handicap was his taciturnity. Also, Wavell, as C-in-C India, did not share Stilwell's strategic optimism for a counter-offensive in Burma so soon after the rout of his forces during the spring of 1942. Additionally, Wavell and Stilwell harboured very disparate views on the use of Chinese troops in Burma. Although this was not stated, Wavell lacked confidence in the Chinese troops offered to him, especially with their loyalty to Chiang Kai-shek. To Wavell, it also seemed correct that British and Commonwealth forces should first and foremost defend an outpost of the British Empire. (USAMHI)

**MAP KEY**

**1** **2 June:** 1st Lancashire Fusiliers and 1st South Staffordshire attack and capture Lakum village and build an airstrip for L-5 aircraft to bring in supplies and evacuate wounded.

**2** **2000hrs, 3 June:** 1st Lancashire Fusiliers takes Loihinche and establishes 77th Indian Infantry Brigade HQ there.

**3** **3 June:** 'Gurkha Village' is captured by 3/6th Gurkha Rifles and an airstrip for L-5 aircraft is built there. Elsewhere, two commando platoons of 1st Lancashire Fusiliers capture Tapaw Ferry east of Lakum on the Mogaung River.

**4** **Early morning, 8 June:** 1st South Staffordshire destroys Japanese ammunition dumps near Pinhmi village.

**5** **Afternoon, 8 June:** 1st Lancashire Fusiliers, passing through 1st South Staffordshire, captures Pinhmi village and moves up to the bridge to await orders.

**6** **Late afternoon, 8 June:** A platoon of 1st Lancashire Fusiliers attempts to work its way along the ditch towards the bridge; one or two of the Fusiliers manage to get onto the bridge itself.

**7** **1800hrs, 8 June:** Calvert meets with Maj David Monteith. The Chindits lay a mortar barrage on the bridge's span and along the Wettauk Chaung's far side, but fail to dislodge any Japanese troops of the entrenched III/114th Infantry. At 1815hrs, after attempting to rush the bridge, Monteith orders his men to withdraw, losing more men on the way back.

**8** **Dawn, 9 June:** Having received word overnight of a ford over the Wettauk Chaung south of the bridge, Calvert attacks with two battalions up, 3/6th Gurkha Rifles and 1st South Staffordshire; leading the attack, the Gurkhas move across the Wettauk Chaung and along a flooded path through the marsh, capturing Mahaung.

**9** **Morning, 9 June:** Maj Frank 'Nip' Hilton's South Staffordshire company attacks and defeats a Japanese party near Ywathitgale. Calvert then dispatches Maj Ron Degg with the rest of 1st South Staffordshire to clear Ywathitgale itself; Degg's men clear Ywathitgale and reach the Pinhmi–Mogaung road. Hearing that Degg's party has reached the Pinhmi–Mogaung road, Calvert orders a company of Gurkhas under Capt G.W.F. 'Fearful' Smith to make demonstrations in order to convince the Japanese that the main Chindit assault would come from Mahaung. Degg's party is directed to build a strong block facing both ways, while Maj Freddie Shaw's men are to attack the Japanese in the rear on the Pinhmi Bridge while the Gurkhas move up from the front; however, it becomes too late for the Gurkhas to attack, and so the attack is postponed.

**10** **Dawn, 10 June:** A Gurkha force commanded by Capt Michael Allmand advances through the marsh; the Gurkhas' initial assault, at 0700hrs, is repelled, but a second attack at 1000hrs successfully captures the bridge.

**11** **Midday, 11 June:** The Chindits capture the court house.

**12** **Midday, 11 June:** The area extending to the Mogaung River and up to the outskirts of Natyigon is cleared of Japanese by Calvert's Chindits.

## Battlefield environment

Mogaung was surrounded by the Wettauk and Namyin *chaungs* to the south-east and west, respectively, and to the north by the wide and swift-flowing (6 knots) Mogaung River, which flowed in an easterly semi-circular direction from the town to the Tapaw Ferry and then to the Irrawaddy. The Wettauk Chaung had a steel-girder road bridge that crossed it at the village of Pinhmi. The Mogaung River just north of the town was bridged by a damaged steel-girder railway bridge on the Myitkyina–Rangoon railway line. Lakum village was in the hills to the south overlooking the Pinhmi Bridge and this was from where Calvert planned his attack against the steel structure over the Wettauk Chaung. Loilaw village was where the railway from Myitkyina to Rangoon crossed the Namyin Chaung, about 4 miles south of Mogaung. Mahaung and Naungkaiktaw

villages were on the west side of the Wettauk Chaung south of the Pinhmi Bridge, and were to be the initial objectives of 3/6th Gurkha Rifles and 1st South Staffordshire, attacking across a ford discovered on 9 June, after the two 1st Lancashire Fusiliers platoons' unsuccessful attempt to storm the bridge on 8 June. Other objectives for 3/6th Gurkha Rifles and 1st South Staffordshire were the court house and railway station.

Exterior of a well-camouflaged Japanese bunker with a narrow firing aperture and foliage camouflage, which made it all but impossible for troops out in the open to direct rifle fire or throw grenades into the position. (USAMHI)

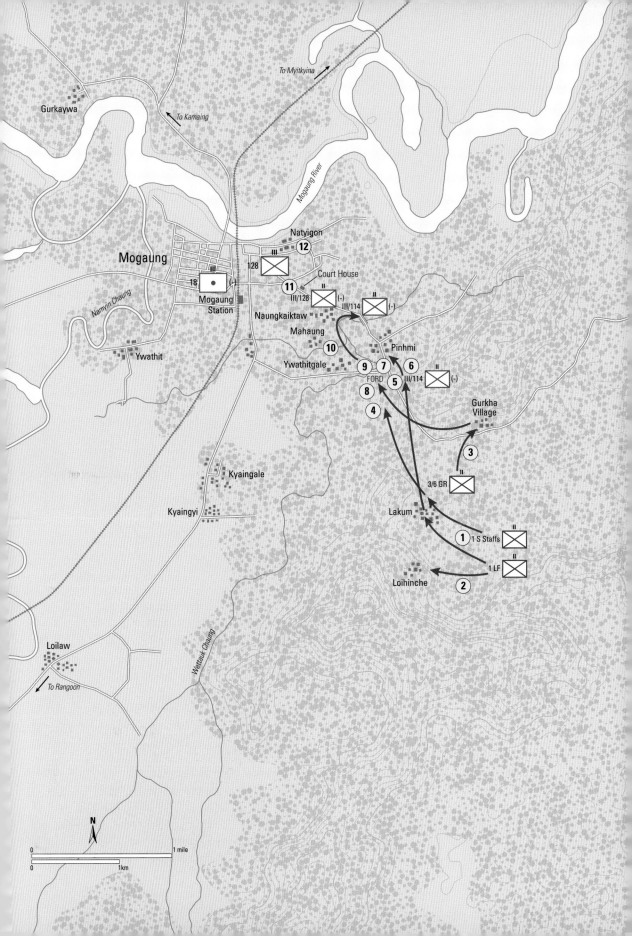

Gurkaywa

To Kamaing

Mogaung River

To Myitkyina

Natyigon

Mogaung

**12**

III 128 [×]

III Court House

18 [×] (-)

Mogaung Station

**11**

III/128 II [×] (-)

II [×] (-) III/114

Namyin Chaung

Naungkaiktaw

Mahaung

Pinhmi

Ywathit

**10**

Ywathitgale

**9** **7** **6**

FORD **5** II [×] (-) III/114

**8**

**4**

Gurkha Village

**3**

3/6 GR II [×]

Kyaingale

Lakum

**1** 1 S Staffs II [×]

Kyaingyi

II [×] 1 LF

Loihinche

**2**

Loilaw

To Rangoon

Wettauk Chaung

N

0                  1 mile

0                  1km

# INTO COMBAT

Leading elements of II/128th Infantry and I/151st Infantry, both of 53rd Division, began to arrive at Mogaung from Myitkyina during the early days of June 1944 to strengthen Mogaung's eastern defences. Calvert's 77th Indian Infantry Brigade would, therefore, encounter a Japanese garrison at Mogaung that was both entrenched and reinforced. Even so, the defenders were in poor shape owing to the environment. As Private Fujino and 2nd Lieutenant Seta, both of II/114th Infantry, made their way from Myitkyina to Mogaung after the capture of the airfield at Myitkyina by Stilwell's forces, two Kachin guides led the Japanese infantrymen through the jungle. Fujino noted:

> We had to go on walking while killing leeches. We could hear hundreds of thousands or might be tens of thousands of leeches dropping down from upper leaves to the lower and over us … I pulled up my sleeves to be able to take off bloody leeches at the moment they attached to the arms. I'd never expected to suffer such combat in a jungle in Burma. (Fujino 1964: 64–65)

After emerging from the jungle, Fujino and Seta

> met three Japanese soldiers in the medical corps. They said, 'We are wandering about to get food for soldiers as the supply is little there … The Burmese never give us food. What is worse, we can't buy anything even if we have money – the military scrip, for they now regard it valueless, just like a piece of paper. The only one way to get food is to exchange it for quinine and we can hardly find the chances.' (Fujino 1964: 68)

After this encounter, Fujino and Seta entered the outskirts of Mogaung: 'We came to a field hospital. It was called "hospital" but it looked like a coarse stable. Under the roof of the palm leaves, soldiers were lying in straw' (Fujino 1964: 68). As elements of III/114th Infantry extricated themselves from the Hukawng Valley on the way to Mogaung, Japanese infantryman Miyashita Susumu observed:

> There was no order to our withdrawal anymore. The jungle and our physical condition was killing us as much as [the enemy]. By now, four of every five men dying in the withdrawal were dying of starvation and disease. Malaria was killing us, too. There was no more discipline. There was no one giving orders. We were in the jungle, and everyone was now on their own … I had been shot twice; once through the shoulder and once through the knee. And every day, as I limped and crawled … I would search for a vehicle with gasoline in it. If I could find one, I would siphon a bit of gas out of its tank with a long cane and use the gasoline to clean my wounds. Otherwise the maggots would grow huge. Gasoline was the only thing that I could find to kill the maggots. My life, every day, had become a struggle to stay alive. (Quoted in Webster 2004: 312)

Mogaung was strongly garrisoned and surrounded by water obstacles, so a direct frontal assault was immediately eliminated as a possibility by the Chindits. According to Lt W.F. Jeffrey of 1st Lancashire Fusiliers, 'We began to receive irritating messages assuring us that Mogaung was only lightly held,

A British 3in mortar crew bombarding Japanese defensive positions in Burma in March 1945. The Chindits' main source of sustained fire support came from the .303-calibre Vickers medium machine gun and the 3in mortar; two of each were retained within each column. As the Japanese assumed a defensive posture in 1944 with strong, fortified bunkers blocking the Chindit advance to Mogaung, such as at Pinhmi Bridge, new tactics were needed to counteract these enemy positions. The 3in mortar crew would fire smoke as well as high-explosive shells to support Chindit infantry assaulting the bunkers. Depending on whether the mortar was a Mk I or Mk II, the range of this weapon was between 1,600yd and 2,800yd. As at Pinhmi Bridge, most of the reinforced Japanese bunkers were impervious even to the 3in high-explosive round, with catastrophic results for the Lancashire Fusilier platoons crossing the Wettauk Chaung to assault the pillboxes dug into the embankment. Aerial assault with P-51 fighter-bombers and better reconnaissance to work around to the rear of the bunkers in order to lob grenades and place explosive satchels would need to be employed to continue the advance. (© IWM SE 3281)

and that we need have no anxiety about capturing at once. Our own intelligence, however, based on villagers' reports, advised us that it was held by about a battalion strength, a large enough defending force in good conditions against troops attacking with artillery support' (Jeffrey 1950: 128). In fact, the Japanese had roughly 3,500 men at Mogaung, comprised of: elements of III/114th Infantry (18th Division); elements of 18th Division's artillery, in Mogaung town; the headquarters of 128th Infantry Regiment (53rd Division); and III/128th Infantry (53rd Division), which had become available as reinforcements for the Mogaung garrison after the Chindit abandonment of Blackpool. There were also various kinds of service troops looking after the ammunition dumps and hospital, along with in-patients in the latter, armed usually with hand grenades as their weapon of last resort.

Calvert decided that his brigade should advance during a battle of attrition against successive Japanese outposts and occupied villages along a narrow east–west line. The Japanese positions were to be reconnoitred, then 'aerial artillery' – usually in the form of P-51 attacks – would be brought to bear on the defenders. This in turn would be followed up by infantry, assaulting behind a mortar barrage and direct Vickers machine-gun fire and tasked with subduing the entrenched Japanese positions with submachine-gun fire, grenades and flamethrowers. As Lt Durant of 1st South Staffordshire stated when summing up some of the infantry assaults, 'I have purposely left out all the descriptions of rotting bodies and dangling guts, because that is a constant factor in war the world over' (quoted in Bidwell 1979: 268). Some Japanese strongpoints were

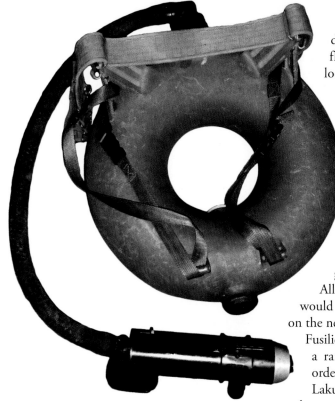

dug in beneath Burmese houses, and for these flamethrowers would be used, since the loopholes were covered with metal grilles to deflect grenades.

Calvert's tactical assault on Mogaung began on 2 June as his brigade advanced from the south-east across 2 miles of open country studded with villages, each one fortified with bunkers dug underneath them and with the capability of covering the front with interlocking fields of fire. In turn, Japanese positions were identified and duly attacked by P-51s; this was followed by Chindit mortar and machine-gun fire, leading to each position's capture by Allied infantry. A village captured in this manner would then serve as the take-off point for the attack on the next fortified village. On 2 June, 1st Lancashire Fusiliers and 1st South Staffordshire, moving along a range of hills to the east of Mogaung, were ordered to attack and capture the sizable village of Lakum, where there were substantial ammunition dumps, a hospital and several HQ units. Jeffrey noted later that as 1st Lancashire Fusiliers approached Lakum, after having had a couple of firefights with Japanese infantrymen attempting to infiltrate the Chindits' bivouac,

A No. 2 'Lifebuoy' flamethrower. The Chindits were equipped with weapons like these to reduce Japanese pillbox defences. Fighting until extermination was commonplace among the infantrymen of 18th Division. Although effective on entrenched enemy combatants, the flamethrower had a limited range, necessitating the operator to get within yards of the bunker – making it an extremely hazardous assignment. (Neil Grant)

The country leading up to Lakum village consisted of a series of hills, covered with thick jungle and intersected with deep ravines. The path was hard to follow and led from hill to hill, sometimes along the side of a ridge and sometimes straight up and down. We had no choice except but to follow it: for to make any detour or short cut through the jungle would have wasted hours and exhausted both men and animals. It was easy country to defend; a handful of resolute men could hold successive hill-tops for hours against a large force such as ours overburdened with mules and heavy stores … The Japanese … could direct a constant stream of bullets down the path from covered positions … The path we were following along a ridge disappeared down a steep ravine and wound its way up the far side between thick trees and undergrowth. For some time, the leading platoon tried to crawl round the Japanese position, meeting heavy and accurate fire, while on the near side of the ravine we unloaded our machine guns and plastered the top of the hill a hundred yards away. At last a Bren gunner in the leading rifle section lost his temper, and rushed straight up the hill, firing from the hip and screaming curses at the Japanese. He was an ordinary soldier who had never been noticed much before. But there is no knowing who in battle will go mad suddenly and leave everybody gasping at his recklessness. (Jeffrey 1950: 130–31)

In Lakum, the Chindits were able to receive regular supply drops and they built a light-aircraft strip to fly out their wounded. From Lakum, Pinhmi – where a steel road bridge took the Tapaw Ferry–Mogaung road over the

30yd-wide, flooded and unfordable Wettauk Chaung to the east of Mogaung – was seen as the next step forward. According to Jeffrey, 'The advance down the [Lakum] hillside went very slowly. There were several ammunition dumps in the jungle half-way down, and the Japanese fought hard for each one' (Jeffrey 1950: 140). This was a very ominous foreshadowing of the assault across Pinhmi Bridge on 8–10 June. The Pinhmi Bridge attack, carried out by two platoons of 1st Lancashire Fusiliers, would represent a culmination of several days of combat for the Chindits against the Japanese in which the former were utilized outside of their normal role as LRP infantry. Upon reaching the top of a hill in Lakum, Jeffrey gazed upon Mogaung, later noting:

> In fact, we could see no signs of life, let alone troop movements and fortifications. But when I looked again, I noticed how thick the jungle was on the approaches and how many streams and large pools criss-crossed the country. There was enough cover for a couple of divisions … The country was covered with thick bushes, lantana grass and prickly thorn. Water was everywhere, in pools, in chaungs and in bogs … I had thought of Mogaung as a town, but it was in fact little more than a large village consisting of bamboo huts raised three or four feet off the ground on stilts. There was, however, one red-brick building – at the railway station, on the north-east corner – which we guessed rightly that the Japanese would make a strong point in their defence system. (Jeffrey 1950: 134 & 138–39)

Calvert called down P-51 strikes on the town of Mogaung, 2 miles from the ridge line at Lakum, after being fired on by 18th Division's artillery and 6in mortars. Upon receipt of 4.2in mortars, air-dropped on 2 June, the Chindits used them to harass Mogaung's Japanese garrison. On 3 June, Calvert reconnoitred the town of Mogaung; C-47 Dakotas began a supply drop just east of the ridge, and 1st Lancashire Fusiliers took Loihinche and established Brigade HQ there. 1st South Staffordshire and 3/6th Gurkha Rifles were nearby at Lakum. Also on 3 June, two Commando platoons of 1st Lancashire Fusiliers, led by Capt George Butler and stationed to the rear of the brigade, captured Tapaw Ferry on the Mogaung River to ensure that a Chindit escape route to the east was available if required. The settlement called 'Gurkha Village' by the Chindits was seized by 3/6th Gurkha Rifles, and an airstrip for light aircraft was built.

Calvert had decided that, rather than attacking Mogaung directly from the south from the village of Loilaw – the direction from which, he reasoned, the Japanese would expect his assault to come – he would confuse the enemy by putting in an initial attack from the south-east, through flooded marshes and lakes and across Pinhmi Bridge. The Japanese were in excellent concealed positions high up on the 15ft embankment leading to the far side of the bridge.

Early on the morning of 8 June 1944, 1st South Staffordshire destroyed some Japanese ammunition dumps in the vicinity of Pinhmi village, which was defended by some infantrymen of III/128th Infantry (53rd Division), on their way down to the bridge over the Wettauk Chaung. There, 1st South Staffordshire halted to let 1st Lancashire Fusiliers capture Pinhmi village later that day. On the Lancashire Fusiliers' side of the bridge, the road from the village was raised several feet above ground level, with a ditch about 4ft deep choked with grass and bushes on the near side and, on the far side, dense jungle that led to the Mogaung River. As Jeffrey noted, 'The bridge itself was

about ten yards long and twenty feet high: beneath it the ground was a mixture of water and marsh. The Japanese had dug in on the rising ground, just over the bridge, from where they could spray the bridge itself and the road nearly as far as Pinhmi three hundred yards away' (Jeffrey 1950: 141).

At first a Chindit platoon tried, in a *coup de main*, to work its way along the ditch towards the bridge, but it was overgrown and the water was too deep to bring effective fire into the Japanese positions in the embankment on the far side of the bridge. One or two of the Fusiliers did manage to get onto the bridge itself. Jeffrey noted:

> As I approached the position with headquarters, the two companies were lying in the ditch, and farther back in the jungle, out of the areas of the Japanese fire. A Japanese soldier had just been found cowering in a hut, probably in Pin-Mi village [*sic*], and was being kicked along the side of the ditch towards us. He had malaria badly, and was babbling incoherently and waving his arms. He would probably have been kicked to death if Bond, one of the company commanders, had not stopped it. As I came up he bent down to give him water from his own bottle. We sent him back to Brigade under escort. (Jeffrey 1950: 141–42)

At 1800hrs on 8 June, at Pinhmi Bridge Calvert met with the Fusiliers' Maj David Monteith. In the summer evening, the Chindits laid a mortar barrage onto the bridge's span and along the Wettauk Chaung's far side. The mortar barrage did not dislodge any Japanese troops, but an errant round fell short and two Fusiliers were wounded, one being Lt John De Quidt. According to Jeffrey:

> For half an hour a platoon tried to work its way along the ditch towards the bridge, but the jungle was too thick and in places deep in water; nor could they bring fire

A Japanese 7.7mm Type 92 heavy machine gun of the type that was captured after the eventual Allied seizure of Pinhmi Bridge. This gun weighed 62lb and the tripod another 60lb, thus, it was often relegated to a fixed fortification, where the firing position could be changed only by relocating the gun. Being air-cooled, it had distinctive barrel cooling rings. The cartridges had to be oiled before they were inserted. Malfunctions occurred if this procedure was not carried out carefully. Even with these limitations, the Type 92 was the heavy machine gun most often used by Japanese troops between 1941 and 1945. (NARA RG-208-AA-247-D-9)

to bear effectively on the Japanese bunkers. It was even worse on the far side of the road. About six o'clock the Brigadier arrived for a conference, and it was decided that two platoons should attack straight down the road, cross over the bridge and rush the bunkers. We brought up our mortar platoon, and began to bomb the bridge at regular intervals. One of the attacking platoons slipped over the road and lay down in the jungle, the second crouched in the ditch. The mortars were fifty or sixty yards behind them. Gradually the barrage speeded up, until the mortars were firing as fast as they could be loaded. The faces of the men in the ditch were tired and grim: some of them pressing each others' hands. My own belly was turning over and over and tying itself into knots. (Jeffrey 1950: 142)

Not having conducted a proper reconnaissance, the British were unsure whether there were any Japanese, or whether they would be waiting in entrenchments. In fact, the road leading to the bridge was in clear sight of the Japanese who were burrowed into the embankment on the other side. Under the cover of heavy mortaring, two platoons of 1st Lancashire Fusiliers fixed bayonets, climbed out of the ditch and rushed across the bridge to seize the Japanese positions. The Japanese on the river's far side waited until the lead Fusiliers were halfway across the bridge before firing and, with the Chindits out in the open, many began to fall; chaos ensued as a few of the Fusiliers crawled on their bellies along the bridge's surface, trying to push far enough forward to throw hand grenades into the enemy pillboxes, but the Japanese fire was too heavy. At 1815hrs, Monteith ordered a withdrawal. Jeffrey stated:

It was suicidal … For several minutes the platoon tried to get over the bridge, so that they could throw grenades into the bunkers, but they were driven back by fire from positions which could not be seen and which offered small targets. They had to retreat, losing more men on the way back. Some men were driven off the road into

# Assaulting the bridge

**Japanese view:** The Japanese defenders at Pinhmi Bridge were a mixed lot. Some had been in Burma since 1942 and had become sick and debilitated from malnutrition and disease. Fresher troops from 53rd Division had recently reinforced them. The bridge's defenders remain hidden in fortified bunkers and camouflaged rifle pits carved out high on the 15ft embankment above the Wettauk Chaung. The sun is getting lower behind them so they will not have any glare to impair their view amid the interlocking fields of fire that they have previously established. They have suffered casualties from earlier P-51 fighter-bomber attacks and now are relatively assured that the enemy's mortar barrage cannot penetrate their wood- and metal-reinforced bunker roofs. None of the Japanese defenders has been dislodged by the most recent Chindit mortar attack, coinciding with the British soldiers climbing onto the far end of the bridge. Patiently, the Japanese infantrymen wait until the lead Chindits are halfway across the bridge surface before commencing their fire from 6.5mm Type 96 and 7.7mm Type 99 light machine guns. As these are fixed fortifications, both the 6.5mm Type 3 and 7.7mm Type 92 heavy machine guns, weighing roughly 120lb each with their tripods, are also being employed against the British attack. A Type 1 heavy machine gun also sprays the bridge; it is a scaled-down Type 92 weapon, weighing just 81lb. From the rifle pits comes rifle gunfire along with rounds from the 5cm Type 89 grenade discharger, which when fired from the kneeling position in the trench could hurl a 29oz Type 89 high-explosive shell 150–700yd depending on where the infantryman had adjusted the firing pin within the barrel.

**British view:** At 1800hrs, without proper reconnaissance, two veteran platoons of 1st Lancashire Fusiliers, having been in northern Burma for three months, have climbed out of a 4ft-deep ditch choked with grass and bushes on the left side and from dense jungle on the right side of Pinhmi Bridge. Hoisting themselves onto the bridge's road surface, the Fusiliers have fixed bayonets and now charge across the 30yd span, which was raised 20ft above a mixture of water and marsh. The light is fading as dusk approaches, and tall, dense mangrove swamps block the *chaung's* far side. The attackers are unsure whether the Japanese have fled after recent P-51 fighter-bomber raids that preceded their own simultaneous mortar barrage falling on the far embankment, which has further obscured the Chindits' view; or if, instead, the Japanese defenders await them, deeply burrowed in their fortified entrenchments. The Fusiliers run towards the far side of the bridge, well aware of the confining aspect of the bridge's steel girders to either side of them and the complete absence of cover. Once partway across the bridge, the two attacking platoons hear the familiar sound of chattering Japanese machine guns and many of the leading Chindits begin to fall dead or wounded, as a few crawl on their bellies along the bridge's surface in a forlorn push forward to throw hand grenades at the enemy fortifications, but the Japanese fire is too heavy.

the jungle and had to crawl back through water. The day ended sombrely. It was growing dark and we were very tired. We gave up the assault on the bridge and withdrew to Pin-Mi village, under cover of our mortars and machine guns. We collected the wounded into one of the huts in the middle of the village, laying the worst on the floor inside and the rest underneath on the ground. (Jeffrey 1950: 143)

Later that night, the rain ceased and the flooded waters receded somewhat, enabling one of Calvert's patrols to find a ford over the Wettauk Chaung south of the bridge. As dawn broke on 9 June, Calvert attacked with 3/6th Gurkha Rifles and 1st South Staffordshire; the former led the way across the Wettauk Chaung and along a flooded path through the marsh. The Gurkhas surprised the Japanese platoon from III/114th Infantry holding Mahaung, killing 12 and capturing the village. After crossing the *chaung* up to their necks in water, Maj Hilton's South Staffordshire company encountered another group of Japanese infantrymen in a bamboo clump near Ywathitgale and, after some stiff fighting, with repeated counter-attacks by the enemy, finally killed most of them and drove away the rest. Then, Calvert dispatched Maj Ron Degg with the rest of 1st South Staffordshire to clear Ywathitgale itself, which was a Japanese administrative headquarters. Degg's force secured Ywathitgale and reached the Pinhmi–Mogaung road.

For the Mogaung offensive, the previously separate columns of 3/6th Gurkha Rifles were consolidated as one battalion. By midday on 9 June, upon hearing that 1st South Staffordshire had reached the Pinhmi–Mogaung road, Calvert left one Gurkha company under Capt 'Fearful' Smith at Mahaung, whose duty it was to demonstrate that this was from where the main assault on Mogaung was now to emanate. Calvert then ordered Degg to dig emplacements to create a strong block facing Mogaung to the west and Pinhmi Bridge to the east. Operating from 1st South Staffordshire's block, the Gurkhas of Maj Freddie Shaw's company were to attack the Japanese in the rear on Pinhmi Bridge; however, it became too late in the day for the Gurkhas to advance into position for an assault.

At dawn on 10 June, Shaw ordered his Gurkhas to advance through the marsh up to their waists in mud and water, just one bend downstream from

A P-47 Thunderbolt and a P-51 Mustang being serviced off the runway at an airfield in Assam. The P-47 was a rugged fighter-bomber capable of withstanding enemy ground fire. Calvert's liaison officers relied heavily on the P-51s and P-47s to provide close air support to the Chindits during Operation *Thursday*, functioning essentially as 'aerial artillery' in the absence of conventional field guns. On 8–10 June, Calvert repeatedly called in P-51 air strikes against the fortified Japanese bunkers in the embankment above Pinhmi Bridge since the British mortar rounds were frequently ineffective against the reinforced roofs of these IJA entrenchments. In addition to these two fighter-bombers, B-25 Mitchell medium bombers could often make strafing pinpoint attacks on enemy positions very close to the Chindit troops. (USAMHI)

In 1944, with the Sino-American and Chindit assaults interdicting 18th Division's LOC, the Japanese infantryman often had to solely rely on northern Burma's resources for food, resulting in malnutrition and sickness as shown by this 18th Division prisoner captured at Mogaung. His uniform is in tatters and he lacks the usual brown pigskin hobnailed ankle boots with his feet instead wrapped in puttees only. The Japanese soldier was economical and took off his boots as often as possible to prolong the wear on them, but the conditions in the Hukawng and Mogaung valleys – plus the duration of ceaseless campaigning there – destroyed them. Compare this emaciated, ill-appearing soldier with the healthier-looking infantryman captured roughly four months earlier shown on page 54. (USAMHI)

the Japanese entrenchments above the bridge. The Gurkha assault party was under the command of Capt Michael Allmand. Allmand, like Monteith, was a cavalry officer who had joined the infantry, in his case 3/6th Gurkha Rifles. The Gurkhas set upon the bunkered-in enemy from behind with rifle fire and grenades, but the attack was repelled and the Gurkhas had to retreat into the jungle. At 1000hrs, the Gurkhas attacked the Japanese bunkers again from the downstream flank while shooting their rifles and hurling their hand grenades amid the waist-deep mud and dense reeds of the Wettauk Chaung. Finally, the intensity of the Japanese machine-gun fire began to diminish as some of the Japanese positions were neutralized. After a hard fight, the Gurkhas took the bridge, killing about 35 Japanese and capturing one medium machine gun and two light machine guns. Gurkha casualties were heavy; they had taken the Japanese bunkers from behind, which was not easy since the attackers were in open countryside once they emerged from the marsh's waters. The Japanese were in excellent concealed positions high up on the 15ft embankment leading to the bridge, surrounded by a sea of marsh and mangrove swamp. They could never have expected that the Gurkhas could cross the marsh in force other than by the road.

By midday on 10 June, Calvert's brigade was securely established along the axis of the Pinhmi–Mogaung road, with two battalions up and a third in the Pinhmi Bridge area. Chindit casualties in the encirclement and capture of the Pinhmi Bridge were about 130 killed and wounded. The delay in capturing the bridge had given Lieutenant-General Takeda time to bring more men into Mogaung. During the evening of 12 June, the remainder of two new Japanese battalions, II/128th Infantry and I/151st Infantry (53rd Division), arrived at Mogaung from Myitkyina to strengthen the eastern defences of Mogaung town. Soon, four battalions from 53rd Division would be facing Calvert, who was still awaiting his Chinese reinforcements, intended to assist him in the assault on Mogaung. Two days after the capture of Pinhmi Bridge, Allmand led another attack well ahead of his Gurkha company. This gallant leadership style ended on 24 June at Natyigon, the last Japanese outer bastion. Allmand singlehandedly silenced a Japanese machine gun; however, he was hit and fell mortally wounded. He received a posthumous Victoria Cross for his heroism under fire.

Calvert's brigade had attacked Mogaung with a strength of 2,000 men, re-grouped into three battalions, out of the original 3,000 Chindits. They faced over 4,000 Japanese in strongly fortified bunkers and village huts. When the Japanese were finally driven out of Mogaung, Calvert's brigade had suffered over 50 per cent casualties and when Stilwell ordered him to take 77th Indian Infantry Brigade to join the battle at Myitkyina, he had only 300 fit soldiers out of the original 3,000. To the relief of Calvert, Stilwell's Chinese troops arrived on 18 June, along with artillery. Although the Chindits had aerial superiority and used 1st Air Commando Group's resources as 'aerial artillery', ultimately the Chindits' potential as a LRP force was squandered at Mogaung, essentially fighting hut-to-hut and bunker-to-bunker, first in the numerous surrounding villages and then in the town itself.

# Analysis

The campaign in northern Burma in 1943 and 1944 was fought by both sides in some of the worst terrain and conditions of World War II. Both Japanese and British infantry forces were trained harshly, but appropriately, for the challenging Burmese combat theatre. Despite this, the march discipline and fieldcraft methods exhibited by many Chindits during *Longcloth* were poor – in particular, handling of mules, swimming capabilities of the troops (given Burma's extensive waterways) and the logistics of river crossings. The envelopment and encirclement tactics that had served the Japanese so well during the conquest of Burma – based on the simple but effective tactics of surprise and rapid movements – were instilled in all junior Japanese officers. Both sides' forces had to operate at the very end of their LOC and if innovative methods were not developed or protected to ensure adequate delivery of supplies, failure in battle would be imminent. The Japanese had some motor roads and the use of the railway to maintain their garrisons and continue effective patrolling; however, the geographic area for which 18th Division was responsible was enormous. Given the Chindits' complete reliance on RAF resupply, sections equipped with radios, requiring mules to transport them due their weight, were integrated into the columns to co-ordinate parachute supply drops and direct the construction of emergency airstrips, if feasible.

## LESSONS LEARNED: THE BRITISH

During *Longcloth*, Wingate sought to avoid large-scale battles with the Japanese. The Chindit tactical movements of 'feint and thrust' were intended to allow designated columns to slip between Japanese units in western and northern Burma, enabling elements of Calvert's No. 3 Column to reach the Nankan railway and demolish bridges and track in order to disrupt 18th Division's LOC. In 1943, Wingate's credo was that a Chindit column's security was in its mobility and ability to break off from an engagement and rendezvous at a pre-designated locale. The LRP column was essentially company-sized and despite lacking motor transport, Chindit weaponry was quite potent for this newer, more mobile type of guerrilla warfare, as mules often carried the 3in mortars and Vickers machine guns. The battle at Nankan Station on 6 March 1943 proved to be an exception, however. Instead of dispersing when Japanese lorried infantry arrived, Maj Calvert had his ambush parties confront the Japanese patrols while the other Chindits completed their demolition preparation. His position could have been overrun by the Japanese aggressively attacking through Nankan village towards the railway station had it not been for the unexpected arrival of a major part of another Chindit column. Having not incurred any casualties up to that point, Calvert's now-augmented force uncharacteristically attacked the Japanese force as it was advancing and put it to flight. The weaponry employed by the Chindits – Bren light machine guns, 3in mortars and Boys anti-tank rifles – enabled Calvert's ambush parties to prompt the Japanese to dismount from their motor transport and mount a cross-country bayonet charge. It was only after the battle was won for the British that Calvert decided to disperse his men fully and move to the agreed rendezvous point.

At Pagoda Hill on 16–18 March 1944, Calvert – now a brigade commander – imbued the offensive spirit into 77th Indian Infantry Brigade's columns as they marched on Henu from their 'stronghold' at Broadway. The new operational paradigm of the 'stronghold' was pivotal in supplanting the 'disperse and regroup' dictums of 1943. With supply and reinforcement flown in, these 'strongholds' could attract enough attention from the Japanese to constitute virtual offensives on their own. Once Calvert's men came under fire from local Japanese units in disparate locations, the brigadier ordered a bayonet charge – almost unthinkable in Wingate's doctrine – up Pagoda Hill that resulted in a hand-to-hand melee. In fact, upon reaching the hill's apex, Lt Durant noted Japanese entrenchments under the village huts, indicative of a notable tactical shift for the enemy, too.

By early June, Stilwell ordered the remaining Chindits in Calvert's 77th Indian Infantry Brigade to attack Mogaung, essentially as conventional infantry. Calvert underestimated the difficulties of the terrain approaching Mogaung and also the tenacity in defence of the well-fortified Japanese bunkers – cut underneath huts with interlocking fields of fire – in every village that the Chindits had to capture to continue their mission to Mogaung. On 8 June, Calvert needed to cross the Wettauk Chaung over Pinhmi Bridge by direct assault to continue his advance on Mogaung. He committed a major error by not properly reconnoitring the Japanese position at Pinhmi Bridge, which consisted of concealed bunkers and rifle pits looking directly over the bridge. A frontal assault across the open bridge was not only inconsistent with the Chindits' LRP training and mission; in this case it proved lethal for the two Lancashire Fusilier platoons ordered to attack. After the eventual capture of the bridge, 77th Indian Infantry Brigade had to reduce fortified Japanese positions in Mogaung one at a time, operating as conventional infantry in a quasi-urban setting, which bled this once fine brigade 'white'. Special Force had been trained for Operation *Thursday* to lure Japanese troop concentrations into their fields of fire, but now the role was reversed and it took three weeks of savage bunker destruction for the Chindits to reduce Mogaung.

# LESSONS LEARNED: THE JAPANESE

On the Malay Peninsula, the Japanese had successfully employed 'envelopment and encirclement' tactics. During *Longcloth*, once combat commenced the IJA infantryman would press home his attack, as when patrols from Indaw discovered Calvert's demolition parties at Nankan Station. Although the IJA cautioned against the frontal assault, this tactic was employed in the ensuing battle, not only because of the overwhelming desire for the Japanese infantrymen to annihilate the enemy but also because the terrain and the Chindit dispositions precluded the Japanese from mounting an enveloping attack. There was no time for the infantrymen, once disembarked from their lorries under fire, to implement proven methods of infiltration and probing to locate weak sectors, so instead they charged along the Chindit ambush positions' front.

At Pagoda Hill, the Japanese troop dispositions were scattered. The Japanese were prone to execute piecemeal attacks during combat, reducing the chance of success as disparate units mounted assaults at different times without proper co-ordination. After Wingate's airborne campaign and 'stronghold' development spread more widely, Lieutenant-General Kawabe Masakasu, commander of the Burma Area Army, sent 24th Independent Mixed Brigade and part of another division to confront the Chindit forces. Commencing on 6 April, the counter-attack by these units – roughly 20,000 Japanese infantrymen – on Calvert's 77th Indian Infantry Brigade and elements of 3rd West African Infantry Brigade at White City failed. Then, Kawabe rushed the entire 53rd Division, his strategic reserve, to the Mawlu area and it, too, was unsuccessful at ousting the Chindits from their White City 'stronghold'. The failure to wait to concentrate an attacking force against the enemy was a pervasive error made by the Japanese. Also, significant Chindit troop dispositions during Operation *Thursday*, in different locales along the railway in northern Burma, had diluted the customary Japanese concentration of troop and air strength to overwhelm their enemy. A similar example of this tactical error was the piecemeal attacks against the US Marines' perimeter covering Henderson Field on Guadalcanal during the summer and

Japanese infantry cross a Burmese river alongside a bridge that has been destroyed during the Allied withdrawal. Part of the doctrinal training of the Japanese infantryman was to maintain a high-tempo advance and rapidly overcome obstacles, as shown here, which enabled them to employ their envelopment tactics. During the Chindit operations of 1943 and 1944, this impulse – to continue the advance urgently, despite impediments, in order to surround the enemy – persisted. However, Chindit tactics counteracted the Japanese infantry's ability to do so. These were not the British and Indian troops of 1942. During Operation *Longcloth*, Chindit columns would disperse and regroup rather than become surrounded in a firefight by rapid IJA flanking manoeuvres. In contrast, during Operation *Thursday*, Chindit forces would remain within the safe perimeters of their 'strongholds' to confront the rapid assembly of IJA ad hoc infantry formations that typically mounted hurried counter-attacks on the Chindit forces. (USAMHI)

autumn of 1942. Continually pulling one formation to reinforce a failed Japanese attack repeatedly compromised offensive efforts on other fronts.

At Mogaung, for the attack on Pinhmi Bridge the Japanese soon found themselves on the defensive – despite their hatred of it – tactically, operationally and strategically. Although the IJA infantrymen despised the defensive tactic in the early war years, attrition, disease, lack of reinforcements and ammunition shortages compelled the Japanese to fight from carefully prepared concealed fortified entrenchments. The IJA infantryman had proved to be masterful at camouflage and was highly effective in these defensive positions. The defensive tactics were based on the employment of heavy machine guns in fortified bunkers impervious to 77th Indian Infantry Brigade's mortar rounds, and they were protected by light-machine-gun crews and riflemen, also armed with grenade dischargers, burrowed deep into sandbagged pits. Chindit infantry only detected some of these positions in Mogaung when they came under direct fire from them at close range. Too often, bunker reduction would require direct heavier artillery fire, fighter-bomber attack or – as at Pinhmi Bridge – small groups of infantry getting behind the positions to eliminate them with hand grenades or explosive satchels.

In retrospect, many of the Japanese commanders would later acknowledge that 18th Division was spread too thinly. From December 1944 Lieutenant-General Numata Takazo was Chief of Staff of Southern Army, which comprised most of South East Asia. When asked to what extent did Wingate's airborne forces upset the Japanese plan for Operation *U-Go* against Imphal and Kohima, or 18th Division's resistance against Stilwell in the Hukawng or Mogaung valleys, he answered:

> The advance of the airborne forces did not cause any change in Japanese operational plans on either the Central Assam front or the Northern Combat Area Command [NCAC] front. Operations continued accordingly but these airborne forces proved to be a devastating factor in cutting lines of communication. The difficulty encountered in dealing with these airborne forces was ever a source of worry to all the headquarters staffs of the Japanese army, and contributed materially to the Japanese failure in the Imphal and Hukawng operations. (Quoted in Calvert 1996: 289)

Lieutenant-General Naka Eitaro, Chief of Staff of Burma Area Army in 1943–44 and later GOC 18th Division, commented, 'This airborne operation … completely cut off 18 Division's (opposing General Stilwell) supply route, thereby making impossible that division's holding operation against the enemy in North Burma' (quoted in Calvert 1996: 289). Thus, the Japanese leadership in Burma recognized that Wingate had adhered to the original task that he was given at the Quadrant Conference in Quebec during August 1943 – namely to help Stilwell with his Chinese–American forces to take Mogaung and Myitkyina, enabling the Allies to re-establish a land-based communication to China's south-western provinces by road, and thus keep China in the war.

# Aftermath

The task assigned to the Chindits for Operation *Thursday* was to assist Stilwell's Sino-American forces to take Mogaung and Myitkyina, by disrupting the LOC for 18th Division in the Hukawng and Mogaung valleys. In retrospect, many of the Japanese commanders acknowledged that 18th Division was spread too thinly. Initially, Mutaguchi was dismissive of *Longcloth*'s aims and accomplishments, although, it did convince him that he could march his army westwards to India across the Chindwin. However, by 1944, the simultaneous operations of *U-Go* and *Thursday*, coupled with the Sino-American offensive from Ledo in late 1943, would devastate the 18th Division's presence in the Hukawng Valley.

Four P-51 fighter-bombers fly low over Hailakandi airfield, while a B-25 Mitchell medium bomber taxis on the ground. These aircraft of 1st Air Commando Group provided Wingate with 'aerial artillery' offering highly accurate fire support. The P-51 had a dual function as a bombing and strafing aircraft.
(© IWM EA 20833)

A 25-pdr Mk I crew fires their field artillery piece against the Japanese. This weapon was vital in defending the Chindit 'strongholds', such as those at Broadway and White City. After the victory at Pagoda Hill on 16–18 March 1944 enabled Calvert's columns to construct the White City 'stronghold', 2-pdr anti-tank guns, Bofors anti-aircraft guns and a battery of 25-pdrs were flown in on 29 March. The 25-pdr gun was vital in breaking up massed IJA infantry assaults and could also disrupt troop assembly areas since it could fire high-explosive shells in addition to smoke and armour-piercing rounds. Additionally, the 25-pdr was a capable counter-battery weapon against Japanese guns brought up as part of 24th Independent Mixed Brigade's all-out attack against White City that commenced on 6 April. Although the airstrips at Chindit 'strongholds' served these fortified bases well, when the monsoons commenced, their continued use became problematic owing to lack of all-weather surfaces. At the beginning of May, Aberdeen was abandoned, followed a few days later by Broadway and White City. (© IWM SE 275)

A Chindit infantryman searches for weapons hidden in the dishevelled uniforms of some Japanese prisoners captured after close-quarters fighting for Mogaung. Often the Japanese prisoners were stripped to just a loincloth to make it easier to detect hidden weapons, such as hand grenades. The Japanese warrior code compelled many prisoners, even if wounded, to attack their captors in order to die honourably in a combative role. (USAMHI)

As the second Chindit operation was just beginning, the Japanese Operation *U-Go* into Assam in March 1944 would seal the fate of Tanaka's 18th Division, which would now have to combat the Allied forces in northern Burma with fewer supplies and limited reinforcements, ultimately leading to the eventual destruction of this once-dominant division as it assumed a purely defensive tactical doctrine. This was the antithesis of Japanese tactics in 1942–43 – encirclement of the enemy and infantry attacks – but now, fortified river lines and concealed jungle bunkers became the norm. Initially, the Japanese infantrymen, due to their stout jungle and river defences, were able to stall the

advance of Stilwell's Chinese troops. However, the dearth of supplies and reinforcements, along with battle casualties – due to both Mutaguchi's offensive and Wingate's interdiction of the railway and roads with his 'strongholds' and blocks – devastated Tanaka's forces. They now took the only feasible strategy, which was to retreat slowly down the Hukawng and Mogaung valleys while hoping that the monsoon would turn northern Burma's rudimentary roads south to Kamaing into a quagmire, thereby bringing Stilwell to a halt. Malnutrition became rampant and many IJA infantrymen could no longer function on a meagre diet of yams and bamboo sprouts.

After five months of fighting behind enemy lines under appalling conditions while conducting operations of an increasingly conventional nature against some of the best IJA formations during Operation *Thursday*, the exhausted survivors of Special Force were evacuated to India. Against Wingate's pre-invasion timetable and beliefs, the time they spent in the Burmese jungles and towns was too long. They were afflicted by battle casualties, disease and malnutrition just like their Japanese counterparts. In February 1945, Special Force was officially disbanded and Admiral Lord Louis Mountbatten, commander of South East Asia Command, lamented: 'It was the most distasteful job in my career to agree to [the] disbandment. I only agreed because by that time the whole Army was Chindit-minded' (quoted in Calvert 1965: 202). Some of this had to do with Wingate's untimely death in late March 1944, depriving Special Force of their champion as well as his direct access to and support from high places to reinforce the tenets of the LRP mission.

# ORDERS OF BATTLE

## Nankan Station, 6 March 1943

### Elements of No. 3 Column (Maj Michael Calvert)
No. 1 Party (Maj Michael Calvert)
No. 2 Party (Capt George Silcock)
No. 3 Party
No. 4 Party (Subadar Kum Singh Gurung)
No. 5 Party (Capt Roy McKenzie)
No. 6 Party (Capt William 'Taffy' Griffiths)

### Japanese forces at Nankan Station
Elements, I Battalion, 55th Infantry Regiment (Major
Shigemi Nagano)


## Pagoda Hill, 16–18 March 1944

### 77th Indian Infantry Brigade (Brig Michael Calvert)
No. 25 Column (Brig Michael Calvert)
No. 36 Column (Lt-Col Hugh Skone)
No. 38 Column (Lt-Col G.P. Richards)
No. 63 Column (Maj Freddie Shaw)
No. 80 Column (Maj Ron Degg)

### Japanese forces at Pagoda Hill
Two companies from a railway-engineer battalion plus
assorted administrative troops
Three sections of a platoon (2nd Lieutenant Kiyomizu) from
II Battalion, 51st Infantry Regiment (Major Takemura)
Nagahashi Unit (Lieutenant-Colonel Nagahashi Jiroku): two
infantry companies formed from units of 18th Division

## Mogaung, 2–10 June 1944

### 77th Indian Infantry Brigade less Nos 81 and 82 columns (Brig Michael Calvert)
Brigade HQ (No. 25 Column)
1st Battalion, The Lancashire Fusiliers (Maj David
Monteith): Nos 20 and 50 columns
1st Battalion, The South Staffordshire Regiment (Maj Ron
Degg): Nos 38 and 80 columns
3rd Battalion, 6th Gurkha Rifles (Col Claude Rome): Nos 36
and 63 columns

### Japanese forces at Mogaung
Elements of III Battalion, 114th Infantry Regiment (Colonel
Maruyama Fusayasu) at Myitkyina
Elements of 18th Division artillery (Lieutenant-General
Tanaka Shinichi) in Mogaung town
HQ, 128th Infantry Regiment
Elements of III Battalion, 128th Infantry Regiment
Service troops looking after the ammunition dumps and
hospital, along with in-patients in the latter

Admiral Lord Louis Mountbatten addresses troops of 7th Battalion,
The Nigeria Regiment (3rd West African Infantry Brigade) in India's
Central Provinces prior to Operation *Thursday*. To Mountbatten's left
is Maj-Gen Wingate and to the left of the photograph, the brigade
commander, Brig A.H.G. Ricketts. After the Quadrant Conference in
Quebec during the summer of 1943, a new organization, the South
East Asia Command, with Mountbatten as Supreme Allied
Commander, was established and encompassed Burma, Malaya,
Sumatra, Ceylon, Siam and French Indochina. Mountbatten, who
previously had headed Combined Operations in the European
theatre, was an enthusiast of special forces and a frequent visitor to
both Wingate's and Stilwell's training sites before the 1944
operation commenced. (USAMHI)

# BIBLIOGRAPHY

Allen, Louis (2000). *Burma: The Longest War 1941–45.* London: Phoenix Press.

Bidwell, Shelford (1979). *The Chindit War: Stilwell, Wingate and the Campaign in Burma: 1944.* New York: Macmillan.

Bierman, J. & Smith, C. (1999). *Fire in the Night: Wingate of Burma, Ethiopia, and Zion.* New York, NY: Random House.

Burchett, W.G. (1944). *Wingate's Phantom Army.* Bombay: Thacker.

Calvert, Michael (1965). *Fighting Mad.* London: The Adventurers Club.

Calvert, Michael (1996). *Prisoners of Hope.* Barnsley: Pen & Sword.

Chinnery, Philip D. (1997). *March or Die.* Shrewsbury: Airlife Publishing.

Chinnery, Philip D. (2010). *Wingate's Lost Brigade. The First Chindit Operation 1943.* Barnsley: Pen & Sword.

Diamond, J. (2012a). *Archibald Wavell.* Oxford: Osprey Publishing.

Diamond, J. (2012b). *Orde Wingate.* Oxford: Osprey Publishing.

Fujino Hideo (1964). *Raft of Death: The Siege of Myitkyina, North Burma.* Carlisle, PA: United States Army Military History Institute.

Gibney, Frank, ed. (1995). *Senso: The Japanese Remember the Pacific War.* Armonk, NY: Sharpe.

Hastings, Max (2011). *Inferno.* New York, NY: Alfred A. Knopf.

Jeffrey, W.F. (1950). *Sunbeams like Swords.* London: Hodder & Stoughton.

Nunneley, J. & Tamayama, K. (2000). *Tales by Japanese Soldiers of the Burma Campaign 1942–1945.* London: Cassell.

Rolo, Charles J. (1944). *Wingate's Raiders.* London: George G. Harrap & Co. Ltd.

Sáiz, Agustín (2011). *Heitai: Uniforms, equipment & personal items of the Japanese soldier, 1931–1945.* Madrid: Andrea Press.

Smith, Colin (2006). *Singapore Burning.* New York, NY: Penguin Books.

Stibbe, Philip (1997). *Return via Rangoon.* Barnsley: Pen & Sword.

Thompson, Julian (2003). *The Imperial War Museum Book of the War in Burma 1942–1945.* London: Pan Books.

Thompson, Robert (1989). *Make for the Hills.* London: Leo Cooper.

Tsuji, Masanobu (1997). *Japan's Greatest Victory. Britain's Worst Defeat.* New York, NY: Da Capo Press.

Warren, Alan (2007). *Britain's Greatest Defeat.* London: Hambledon Continuum.

Webster, Donovan (2004). *The Burma Road.* New York, NY: Perennial Publishers.

Japanese soldiers ascend the slopes of some Burmese mountains in March 1943 in pursuit of the Chindits during the initial raid into Burma, Operation Longcloth. Headgear includes field caps with sun flaps. The Japanese infantrymen were quite adept at traversing harsh terrain such as this, unlike the typical British or Indian soldier during the rout of 1942. Note that the lead infantryman is wearing his hinomaru, or 'flag of the rising sun', as a sling for this right arm. On the eastern side of the Irrawaddy River, it was quite arid and the terrain had some motor roads, which the Japanese used to converge on Wingate's Chindits as they were retreating to re-cross the Irrawaddy and head west for the Chindwin River and, then, Assam. Clearly, Wingate had violated his own tactical tenet and could not use the jungle for concealment when he crossed the 'great' river after the railway was demolished at Nankan and other locales. (USAMHI)

# INDEX

Figures in **bold** refer to illustrations.